When Your Mom Is Autistic

When Your Mom Is Autistic

A Guide to Understanding, Accepting, and Appreciating Your Autistic Mother

Dr. Meghan G. Graham, EdD, CCC-SLP

ADAMS MEDIA
New York Amsterdam/Antwerp London Toronto Sydney/Melbourne New Delhi

adamsmedia

Adams Media
An Imprint of Simon & Schuster, LLC
100 Technology Center Drive
Stoughton, MA 02072

The authorized representative in the EEA is Simon & Schuster Nederland B.V., Herculesplein 96, 3584 AA Utrecht, Netherlands. info@simonandschuster.nl

First Adams Media trade paperback edition October 2026

Interior design by Maya Caspi
Images © Simon & Schuster, LLC

Manufactured in the United States of America

1 2026

Library of Congress Control Number: 2026939092

ISBN 978-1-5072-2553-0
ISBN 978-1-5072-2554-7 (ebook)

Dedication

For my daughters, Lyla and Lucy, who are at the center of every decision I make and every dream I chase. I hope this work reminds you that love does not always look the same, but it can still be deep, steady, and true.

Acknowledgments

To my family—my mom, dad, and Tim—thank you for your constant love, encouragement, and unwavering support throughout every chapter of my life. I would not be here without you.

And to the Autistic women who trusted me with your stories—thank you for allowing me into your lives with such honesty and vulnerability. Your insight, authenticity, humor, strength, and humanity shaped this book in ways I will never fully be able to express. You are beautiful, deeply human, and deserving of a world that understands and values you exactly as you are.

Contents

Preface

For more than twenty years, I have worked as a speech-language pathologist, and during that time I have had the privilege of working with countless Autistic individuals and families. In many ways, they have taught me as much as I have ever taught them. Through their stories, their challenges, and their strengths, I have learned how differently people experience the world and how important it is to approach those differences with curiosity and respect. Over the years, these experiences have shaped how I think about autism, communication, and what it truly means to support people in ways that honor who they are.

Most often, conflict within families stems from a misunderstanding of another person's experiences or intentions. For Autistic women—and especially Autistic mothers—this misunderstanding runs particularly deep.

Through my clinical work, teaching, and research, I have met many Autistic women whose experiences rarely appear in textbooks, diagnostic descriptions, or traditional clinical training. Many spent years—sometimes decades—trying to understand themselves in systems that were never designed with them in mind. Autism research and diagnostic frameworks have historically been based largely on men's presentations of autism. As a result, many Autistic women have been overlooked, misdiagnosed, or left to navigate healthcare and educational systems that struggle to recognize their experiences.

Though I'm a faculty member at Boston University, some of the most important learning in my career has not come from textbooks or lectures. It has come from listening. Several years ago, I began facilitating a group for Autistic women through the speech-language clinic at Boston University's Sargent College. What began as a small clinical program quickly became something much more meaningful. The women who participate in this group bring remarkable honesty, insight, humor, and kindness to conversations about autism, identity, relationships, work, burnout, and the everyday realities of navigating a largely neurotypical world.

Spending time in this community has reinforced something that has become central to my work: If we want to understand autism, we must listen to Autistic people themselves. While I am not Autistic myself, it is important to me that Autistic voices be at the center of conversations about autism, particularly when we are trying to understand the experiences of Autistic mothers. That's why you'll see quotes from Autistic moms throughout this book.

When Your Mom Is Autistic is written with a specific goal: to help adult children better understand their Autistic mothers. Many children grow up sensing that their parent experiences the world a little differently, but they may not have the language to make sense of those differences. This book is meant to help bridge that understanding with compassion, honesty, and respect.

Throughout this book, I use the terms "women" and "mothers" when referring to Autistic mothers. This language reflects the current research literature, which most often uses these terms when discussing autism in adulthood. At the same time, it is important to acknowledge that the Autistic community includes people across a wide spectrum of genders. This book will use she/her pronouns, but many Autistic individuals identify outside traditional gender categories, and those identities deserve recognition and respect.

Since neurodiversity can shape how relationships are experienced and expressed, it's also important to consider how your own neurotype may play a role in how you approach bonding with your mom. Given that autism is often inherited, you may be Autistic as well. With that in mind, the methods in this book are designed to help your bond with your mom whether you are Autistic or not. If you are Autistic, you may find that some strategies fit well and others don't, depending on your own communication style, sensory needs, or preferences—use what feels clear and manageable for you, and adjust or skip the rest.

The women whose experiences inform this work are thoughtful, insightful, and deeply reflective about their lives. They are also navigating systems that often struggle to understand their needs. They deserve to be better understood.

A Note on Trauma

The advice in this book is not intended for people who have experienced abuse from their parents or mothers. If it feels right for you, individual therapy can be helpful for this kind of emotional or trauma processing, or you might find a neurodiversity-affirming family therapist who works with adult families. These professionals can help support both you and your mother in building lifelong healthy relationship skills.

I remain deeply grateful to the women in our group for their generosity in sharing their experiences and perspectives. Their openness, honesty, and kindness have shaped not only this book, but also how I teach, practice, and approach research.

Again and again, they remind me of something simple but essential: Understanding each other begins with listening.

Introduction

Navigating parental relationships is complicated. If your mother is Autistic, you might find that you need help understanding each other more fully. She might be loving, but inconsistent; attentive, but often overwhelmed; devoted, but sometimes emotionally unavailable. A childhood spent in this environment can be filled with joy and love, but it can also trigger lifelong questions about connection, communication, and emotional needs. If this experience resonates with you, you're not alone.

When Your Mom Is Autistic can help you better understand her neurodivergence and offer a new lens through which to view your relationship—past, present, and future. You can't change the past, but you *can* bring clarity to those memories . . . and create new ones that honor both your needs and your mom's. By respecting her preferences, advocating for yourself, and working together to find common ground, you and your mom can try to meet in the middle and focus on the love you share for one another.

This book draws from current research, lived experiences, and neurodiversity-affirming principles to explore ways to make these stronger and more mindful connections with your Autistic mother. In Part 1, you'll learn about autism itself—its common hallmarks, information about diagnosis, and common myths about the condition. Rather than framing autism as a deficit, we approach it as a difference—a unique way of being in the world. We will then unpack the specific challenges that Autistic women and mothers face, and the gender-specific societal expectations they navigate. In Part 2, we'll examine specific components of a child–Autistic mother relationship, such as verbal communication, executive functioning, and emotional expression, and offer practical ideas for improving your bond. The goal of each chapter in Part 2 is to:

- **Understand** the topic in greater detail. For example, how exactly does autism affect your mother's ability to read social cues? Why is her routine so important to her?
- **Accept** that differences exist and learn ways to foster a healthy relationship despite them, such as sample scripts to open a productive conversation and guidance on setting boundaries.
- **Appreciate** the strengths your Autistic mom has. Recognizing these qualities—whether it's deep empathy, fierce loyalty, or a passionate dedication to the people and causes she loves—can help you reframe some behaviors in a mindful way.

Along the way, you'll hear from other children of Autistic mothers, who share their experiences, suggestions, and stories so you know you aren't the only one going through this. Autistic mothers also share their firsthand, lived experiences, which are both informative and authentic. Hearing from others in this community can offer ideas that might work for you, and also provide support in the form of shared understanding and empathy. You'll also find prompts that invite you to reflect on your past, and topics to raise with your mother to help you two forge a more compassionate and authentic connection.

A few important notes: You don't need to be *sure* your mom is Autistic to keep reading. Many women go undiagnosed, and many others self-identify without a formal label. This book isn't trying to diagnose anyone. Its aim is to give you the tools to better understand your mother's experiences, and reconcile how those experiences shape your relationship.

Whether you're seeking validation, healing, or more peaceful relations, this book can help you reflect on your past, discover empathy, and support a caring connection with your mother. With *When Your Mom Is Autistic*, you can better understand your mother—and yourself—and encourage more harmonious family dynamics.

Part 1

Learning about Autism

Autism Spectrum Disorder (ASD) is a neurodevelopmental difference that affects how people experience and interact with the world. Current research estimates that as many as 3 million US adults are Autistic, though that number is likely higher. According to the World Health Organization, globally 1 in 127 people are Autistic. While neuroscientists are still researching many of the origins and explanations of autism, we do know that Autistic people are as intelligent, caring, and multifaceted as their allistic peers. In this part, you'll learn some basics facts about autism so you are aware of some key aspects of your mother's experience.

We'll also explore how autism presents differently in women. For decades, autism was viewed through a lens focused almost entirely on men, leaving many Autistic women undiagnosed, misunderstood, or mischaracterized. The picture of autism that used to define it—often involving boys with overt social and behavioral concerns—doesn't match the reality for many women and girls. This mismatch has led to widespread underdiagnosis and misdiagnosis of Autistic women, especially those who are intelligent, verbal, and socially aware. The foundational knowledge you discover in Part 1 will set you up to co-create an authentic relationship with your mother.

Chapter 1

What Is Autism?

Before we discuss a parent-child relationship, it's first important to gain a foundational understanding of autism. This chapter will explain what it is, how it's defined, and outline some common characteristics of Autistic people. From repetitive behaviors to sensory sensitivity, you'll discover some of the common traits of autism.

You'll also learn about the diagnostic process—some of which might surprise you—and ways to talk about neurodiversity that respect all people. We'll also explore the most effective supports and accommodations that can help Autistic people exist in a neurotypical world. Finally, we'll explore common myths, like the belief that autism only affects men, or that it always looks the same, and unpack the truths behind them. All this information will help you peel back and identify the many layers of your mother as a human being.

Autism, Defined

Autism, which is referred to as Autism Spectrum Disorder (ASD) in diagnostic language, is a developmental and neurological difference that affects how people interact with others, learn, communicate, and behave. It's called a spectrum because there are many variations in the way it presents.

To establish a formal diagnosis, a medical professional will use the industry standard *Diagnostic and Statistical Manual of Mental Disorders* (*DSM*), which provides criteria such as "challenges with social communication and interactions" (often shortened to SCI) in addition to "restricted and repetitive behaviors and interests" (RRBI). While these elements help shape a framework for diagnosis, they do little to help us understand the differences in presentation of Autistic individuals, especially Autistic women. Let's take a look at some of the more common markers of autism.

Differences in Social Interaction

Differences in social interaction broadly refers to the ways in which Autistic people communicate with other people across various contexts.

Current research points to variations in neurological wiring that lead to these differences. There are also some cognitive-based theories related to social understanding (which are controversial in both the Autistic community and the literature) that attempt to explain these differences.

A Note on Gender Labels

Throughout this book, you will see the terms "mom/mother," "woman," "she/her," meaning those that were assigned female at birth, had the role of "mother" as a caregiver, and/or experienced the majority of their lives as a "girl" and "woman." Using gender binaries is limiting, yet currently the bulk of research is set up to use binary language in that way. We know that women's presentation of autism often looks different and therefore their experience within the world is also different. That is the focus of this book, to help you understand how your mother likely experienced the world and how that impacted you. It should be noted that within the Autistic community, there is a higher incidence of diversity of both gender and sexual identity.

Regardless of the exact cause, *brain differences* make the complex nature of social relations (e.g., reading nonverbal language, integrating cues, sensory differences) function differently for Autistic people. That's why Autistic people might have a different way of:

- Maintaining back-and-forth conversation
- Using or understanding facial expressions and body language
- Sharing or matching emotions
- Building or maintaining relationships or connecting with other people, especially non-Autistic, or allistic, people
- Changing behavior and language based on social situation

It's important to note that these differences are often labeled "challenges" or "difficulties" when Autistic people are trying to communicate with people outside their neurological sphere—it's like a neurotypical person trying to talk to someone who speaks another language or has different cultural traditions. It's understandable that a neurotypical person would face challenges and difficulties in that scenario—likewise, an Autistic person might face challenges navigating a social structure built for a neurotypical person. In Chapter 2, we'll talk more about a concept called the Double-Empathy Theory, which highlights the idea that *both* parties are responsible for bridging any gaps in communication style.

A Child's Perspective

"I didn't understand that autism could look like my mom—consistent, quiet, always present but emotionally distant. I thought autism was something loud and obvious. Looking back, I see how deeply I misunderstood what it really is."

—Alina, 31

Restricted and Repetitive Behaviors and Interests (RRBI)

Another hallmark of autism is a person's likelihood to have a unique approach to their interests and routines. These behaviors exist because of unique brain wiring, and they often allow for self-soothing or regulating for Autistic individuals as they navigate a stressful world that isn't designed for them. For example, they might:

- Enjoy repetitive motions
- Thrive on sameness, routines, or consistency
- Fixate strongly on their interests
- Maintain strong sensory preferences (more on that next)

These preferences might show themselves as your mother liking clear "rules" and patterns. Maybe she eats the same things every day. Maybe she has *very* strong interests (often called special interests or enthusiasms), whether it be word origins, animals, or Dungeons & Dragons. These special interests are important for Autistic identity, regulation, and joy. The bottom line is that the presentation of Autistic behaviors and habits will look different in each person, but you will usually notice very strong preferences.

Sensory Sensitivity

Your sensory processing system manages how input from the world around you—such as sounds, lighting, touch, smells, and tastes—is filtered, absorbed, and responded to. Sensory sensitivity refers to having a highly responsive sensory processing system, and most Autistic people experience this situation. Sensory sensitivity is often described as hyper- (high) or hypo- (low) sensory sensitivity. Like the other differences mentioned about Autistic brains, sensory processing differences are a result of neurology and connectivity. How the brain filters, responds, and processes input is different in Autistic people.

Sensory sensitivity can show up in many ways, such as the following:

- Preferring to filter out fluorescent lighting, both in a visual and auditory (buzzing) sense.
- Navigating sounds in spaces like open offices or restaurants, where overlapping conversations and music can be extremely dysregulating or make auditory processing more challenging.
- Noticing visual details and being very focused on them (e.g., asymmetries, patterns).
- Delayed recognition of pain, hunger, or thirst.

What Is Dysregulation?

Dysregulation occurs when a person's body or mind is unable to balance their nervous system properly. Physical dysregulation can include difficulty balancing energy levels, temperature, movement needs, and even heart rate. Emotional dysregulation can show up as mood swings, overwhelm, outbursts, and impulsive behavior.

Sensory preferences are different for all Autistic people—and all people in general. The key difference is that in Autistic people, sensory preferences have a significant effect on daily life. Maybe you observe your mom rocking back and forth to regulate herself. Maybe she feels overwhelmed by loud noises or busy environments. Autistic women sometimes have a hard time recognizing when they are overloaded from a sensory perspective, and then find themselves physically or emotionally dysregulated. Or they may try to "push through" sensory processing overwhelm without truly addressing it, which can lead to dysregulation and a need to withdraw and recharge later.

Difficulty Accessing Executive Functioning Skills

Executive functioning (EF) is essentially the process of completing tasks. It includes memory, attention and focus, planning, executing, time management, and even task switching. To complete a task, you must first figure out how to accomplish the goal: break it down into steps, establish how long each task will take, problem-solve when something doesn't go as planned. For example, to go to the dentist, you have to call the dental practice, check your calendar, schedule the appointment, add it to your calendar, plan how to get there, adjust your work schedule, know how long it will take to get there, attend the appointment, and get back home or to work.

For many Autistic individuals, EF skills do not come easily. Some differences with EF skills exist because of unique brain wiring. Other Autistic people have strong EF capabilities, but have a harder time accessing them at certain moments given the other demands of existing in a neurotypical world. Their physical and cognitive energy has been spent on other tasks, and they don't have enough left to tackle high-demand activities that require EF focus.

What's Involved in a Diagnosis

In a perfect world, a parent notices differences about their child and reports these differences to the pediatrician. The pediatrician will listen, correctly interpret the information, and refer the family to the appropriate professionals (e.g., a developmental pediatrician, a neuropsychologist, a comprehensive team of professionals at a hospital) so that the child can receive a diagnosis early (age three or younger) and can then get the support they need.

Unfortunately, this perfect pathway is rarely followed. Instead, many Autistic people—especially girls and women—find that their journey toward learning more about themselves takes a very different route. For example, they might be misdiagnosed (more than once) or discover they have autism way past childhood, even into middle age. The following are some of the obstacles and wrong exits that this trip can take.

Why Are Women Diagnosed Later?

On average, an Autistic female is diagnosed four times less often than an Autistic male. She is also more likely to be diagnosed at an older age. According to a study published by Epic Research in 2024, 12 percent of Autistic males were diagnosed as adults (age nineteen or older), while 25 percent of Autistic females were diagnosed at that age. There are a few reasons that women are often diagnosed later than men—that is, if they're diagnosed at all. Let's look at some of the factors.

Diagnostic Criteria Were Built Around Men's Presentation of Autism

The diagnostic criteria we discussed earlier in this chapter are based mainly on the presentation of autism in men. What is used to define autism, such as overt social and behavioral concerns, doesn't match the reality for many women and girls. Women are often told, "You don't have autism; you're too social!" or, "It can't be autism; you're too smart." Oftentimes, autism isn't even suggested as a possibility for a woman, because historically society assumed that most Autistic people were men.

A Mom's Perspective

"A late diagnosis answers one question and detonates dozens more. . . . The person I thought I was turned out to be a carefully assembled collection, like a bird picking up shiny pieces over decades, stitching a self from other people's mannerisms, ways of speaking, ways of moving through a room. . . . I can spot a

pattern in a system or a room before anyone else notices, and in the same breath be blindsided by a social cue everyone else received without thinking."
—Mary, 53

Additionally, some Autistic women have been directly told that they aren't Autistic. Even well-meaning people who love them sometimes insist they simply don't seem like they are Autistic. This opinion can also come from people in their professional world who haven't experienced what autism can look like in women. This experience can be incredibly confusing and frustrating for those women.

Familial Diagnosis

Many women are diagnosed after their own child's diagnosis. Given that autism is highly hereditary, this situation makes sense. As they go through the process of observing and hearing from others the ways in which their child may not be thriving in preschool or school, they start to ask questions of themselves: "Did I experience the world in the same ways as a child? Do I too have strong sensory preferences? What were my friendships like?"

In reflecting on their own experiences both throughout their childhood and in their current life, as well as trying to understand their own child, they often then start putting the pieces together. They start realizing that the ways in which their child is experiencing the world feels quite familiar. This self-reflection often jump-starts their journey toward an autism diagnosis, whether that's done in a formal medical setting or via self-diagnosis.

Masking/Camouflaging

Masking is the process of working hard to inhibit and hide Autistic behaviors in order to more easily fit into neurotypical society. There is conflicting data around masking in terms of gender differences—however, women tend to "score higher" on masking behaviors than men do, meaning they mask more often and more convincingly, often without noticing they're doing it. That may be because women can often be better at social imitation and are more socially motivated than men. Again, there are a lot of differences in Autistic presentation, but it's generally accepted that women are much more likely to mask.

We'll talk a lot more about masking in other areas of this book, but for now it's important to know that this tendency can mean that characteristics of autism go unnoticed by medical professionals and other people around Autistic women.

Common Misdiagnoses

In addition to being diagnosed later in life, women are also more likely to be misdiagnosed before they learn they have autism. Autistic people often receive a number of diagnoses before they get to autism, and this is especially true of women. The majority of these women carry diagnoses such as anxiety, depression, OCD, disordered eating, attention-deficit/hyperactivity disorder (ADHD), borderline personality disorder, or even bipolar disorder. While some of these issues may indeed be present, if unrecognized autism is *also* at play, these women don't have the full picture of their health and well-being. These under- or misdiagnoses can lead to a lot of pain, confusion, and misunderstanding.

A Mom's Perspective

"I had an inaccurate list a mile long of diagnoses. I had struggled for a long time, and was even told at one point that I had schizotypal disorder, a mood/personality disorder. I lived my entire childhood and early adulthood thinking that I had so many things 'wrong' with me. I took lots of medications. I had lots of different therapists to help me cope or gain skills for my 'disorders.' I even had to leave college . . . not because I didn't have the academic skills, but rather because I didn't understand my learning and social profile. I didn't understand myself and neither did anyone around me."

—Pam, 47

The Prevalence of Self-Diagnosis

A common and acceptable practice within the adult autism community is self-diagnosis. This may be surprising to people who are used to official diagnoses only coming from trained medical professionals. But given that many medical professionals don't have experience with the presentation of autism in women, self-diagnosis is often the best way for these women to understand themselves. They have often been misdiagnosed or sidelined by these professionals if they did seek a diagnosis, and told again and again that they "aren't Autistic." Through careful self-analysis and reflection, women often come to the diagnosis on their own and take control of their own identity.

Even after they diagnose themselves, women also often seek support outside the medical establishment. They join support groups, read books, seek out Reddit threads, and visit other online communities and forums to discuss their lived experiences with like-minded peers where they can ask questions in a safe space and try to learn more about themselves. Within these communities, they can often get the answers they have been searching for throughout their lives. These resources can:

- Connect them with other people who can validate and relate to their lived experiences.
- Refer them to vetted professionals who may better understand them.
- Recommend supports and accommodations.
- Teach them how to advocate for the care that they need.

Though it may feel unorthodox to some, this self-diagnosis and self-support process works well for some people because it allows for self-discovery and encourages personal agency.

Does a Diagnosis Matter?

Given the prevalence of self-diagnoses and challenges navigating the established medical community, I get asked all the time: "Does my mom even need the diagnosis? If we are open and accepting of neurodiversity, does the actual autism diagnosis make a difference?" The answer is that it's really personal and different for everyone.

- Some individuals are happy with just using the general umbrella label of "neurodivergent."
- Others don't want any label at all, and are understandably worried about issues like parental rights and societal stigma.
- Still others really want to just "know."

In general, many Autistic individuals I have worked with find comfort in officially knowing their diagnosis. For some, initially, it can come with some feelings of shock, heaviness, and grief. Questions arise, such as "Why didn't someone discover this sooner? What if someone had? How would my life be different?" This makes sense given the challenges that most Autistic people experience living in a neurotypical world. Add in elements of societal stigma, gender roles, and how we are socially conditioned to think about Autistic people, and it can all be quite complicated for them to process.

What If You Don't Know If Your Mom Is Autistic?

Some of you might be at a stage where you are wondering if your mom fits into this diagnosis. First, this book is not written with the intent of trying to diagnose anyone. That said, the information you learn from this book can still help you better understand your mom and better love her. If you are questioning this diagnosis with your mother, like most things, it's a personal decision whether or not you want to raise the topic with her. If you decide to do so, given that most Autistic people prefer direct communication, it may help to be just that: direct. You could say something like, "Mom, I've been reading a lot about the presentation of autism in women. Do you know much about this?" Using a very open-ended question like that reduces pressure, and your mother's response will likely tell you quickly whether or not she's open to the conversation. If she's not, that's okay. You can always keep using the tools in this book to try and better understand and connect with her anyway.

What tends to happen more often than not is that diagnosis brings a sense of comfort in finally being able to understand why things have been so hard. Often diagnosis leads to women finding communities of other women who have similar life experiences, which can bring peace and continued understanding. In some cases, an official diagnosis from a medical professional can also open doors to certain legally protected accommodations in structured settings, like workplaces and schools.

Talking about Neurodiversity and Autistic People

It's important to think about the language we use to describe autism and Autistic people. The medical community and society at large have often tended to use negative words like "difficulty," "struggle," "deficit," and "challenges" to describe Autistic behaviors. Yet those words don't always resonate with the experience of many Autistic people.

The Origin of the Term "Neurodiversity"

In the 1990s, Australian researcher and sociologist Judy Singer coined the term "neurodiversity." Her thesis suggested autism and other conditions like ADHD and dyslexia are just normal variations of the brain. She believes that we are simply all wired differently and that fact is important to understand and celebrate. She likens neurodiversity to the importance of biodiversity in nature, saying that they both make the world a better place. As she states, "Why not propose that just as biodiversity is essential to ecosystem stability, so neurodiversity may be essential for cultural stability?" She goes on to say that neurodiversity captures the "whole of humanity." Thinking of neurodiverse individuals in this light takes the focus off their differences and "struggles" and names them as a key part of our diverse humanity.

Singer also inspired the neurodiversity movement, a political effort to promote civil rights for neurodivergent people. Today, Singer's paradigm shift in thinking about autism is gaining even more momentum as more Autistic adults speak out about their experiences. It's shifting the narrative away from talking about Autistic people having "deficits" and bringing it toward a strength-based view of life on the spectrum.

Avoid Limiting Language

Speaking of "deficits," society also often describes Autistic people as "low" and "high" functioning, which is quite limiting—and can even feel insulting—to the Autistic community. In the *DSM-5*, Autistic people are described on "levels," which indicate their support needs in a clinical way (level 1: requiring support; level 2: substantial support; and level 3: very substantial support). Outside of a clinical setting, terms like "high support needs" and "low support needs" are more readily used. However, this is quite problematic because they describe people in a simplistic, linear way. Plus, doesn't *everyone* have needs? This language also doesn't account for the variability among Autistic people, and certainly does not capture who they are as a whole person. Consider a person who has incredibly high cognition (thinking, understanding) yet doesn't speak with their voice but rather with a voice output device. What about someone who has strong language skills but can't follow through on tasks like shopping and cooking given their weaker executive functioning (organizing, planning, goal setting) skills? Do those people have high or low needs? It depends on how you look at it. In addition, a person may need "low" or less support to function within this world compared to someone with a more significant cognitive or physical disability, yet they still have very real needs. The bottom line: Trying to describe "high" or "low" needs is difficult, potentially insulting, and probably ultimately inaccurate anyway.

Our Story

I used to think my mom just didn't *want* to connect with me the way other moms did with their kids. After all, she didn't go to school functions. She never seemed to know how I was feeling unless I spelled it out. She sometimes said the "wrong" thing, or nothing at all. I often thought she wasn't interested in me, or was even bored by me.

It wasn't until I had my own child that I started to understand her differently. I was scrolling through a parenting forum one night, exhausted, looking for advice on sensory-friendly spaces and activities and stumbled into a post titled "I Didn't Know I Was Autistic Until I Became a Mom." I read the entire thread multiple times. So much of what these women were saying—about burnout, about needing routines, about feeling overwhelmed and deeply misunderstood—sounded so much like my mother. I had never thought of her that way.

Eventually, I asked her directly, "Do you think you might be Autistic?" She paused and said, "I've wondered. I always felt . . . different." That conversation changed everything.

—Alex, 34

Recognizing Intersectionality

Intersectionality is an important component to consider when evaluating your relationship with your Autistic mother. This model, coined by scholar Kimberlé W. Crenshaw, explains the interconnected nature of social categories like race, class, and gender, and how these categories overlap and build an interdependent system that creates discrimination and disadvantage. Intersectionality can help us better understand the extra complexities that some Autistic people can face.

Intersectionality shows us how social and economic systems can impact the Autistic experience even more than neurology. Black and brown children are diagnosed later than their white peers. When we add in gender, that further complicates diagnosis—Black and brown women are diagnosed later still. Additionally, different cultures recognize disabilities in different ways. Some hold strong beliefs that can be quite stigmatizing for an Autistic person. Many Autistic LGBTQ+ individuals find that their sexuality and/or gender expression affects their Autistic experience as well.

Diagnosis and intervention around autism also requires resources, both in terms of finances and family support. Autistic people without sufficient resources might face extra challenges existing in a neurotypical world. The takeaway here is that identity is *complicated*—every person's lived experience is layered with so many factors.

Reconsidering "Treatment"

The medical model of disability is a way of looking at a person's condition as something that needs to be treated or cured. For autism, this looks like addressing the "deficits" mentioned in the *DSM*. Some historical and current approaches to autism are focused on making Autistic people behave in ways that are considered more "normal" or neurotypical. These plans might include practicing conversation skills, modeling how to ask questions, suggesting appropriate comments, demonstrating typical body language or eye contact, and showing how to stay "on topic." While well-meaning, these treatment ideas come with their share of issues. They are essentially trying to make Autistic people someone they are not.

At their core, these plans aim to fundamentally change the Autistic person, which can cause significant psychological harm. As you can likely imagine, trying to be someone that you are not is not just impossible, it's also dangerous. Both scientific research and personal Autistic experience demonstrate how detrimental this approach is to personal well-being—it leads to low self-esteem, exhaustion, and even suicidality. Imagine if you were asked to have a conversation about things that you have *no* interest in, or to perform specific nonverbal actions in order to communicate with someone. That's how Autistic people sometimes say they feel if they are asked to use neurotypical communication styles. It's so difficult for anyone to act in ways that don't feel natural or comfortable. The cognitive load to try and converse in ways that don't align with how your brain works is exhausting, yet this is what we expect Autistic people to do. "Treatments" often ask them to do something to "fit into" neurotypical expectations of what is "social."

More progressive and modern intervention approaches are called "neurodiversity-affirming." Neurodiversity-affirming methodologies:

- Focus more on the Autistic person's strengths.
- Help people understand and embrace their individual identity.
- Presume competence.
- Can be customized for personal communication preferences.
- Promote agency and self-advocacy to give people what they need.

This collaborative and empowering approach can reduce anxiety around support and improve overall well-being.

Social Disability versus Medical Model

Whereas the medical model views a disability as a medical issue that needs curing, the social model of disability explains that a person's "deficits" are largely caused by society's expectations and judgments, not an actual medical impairment. In other words, the social model posits that society creates the disability by setting up barriers that prevent the person from participating fully. These could be physical, such as lack of wheelchair access; sensory, such as the common presence of bright overhead lighting; or social, such as how people label eye contact or small talk as "professional behavior."

Myths versus Truths

Stereotypes and media depictions of autism have led to many pervasive myths about the condition. Dismantling these myths can help you see your relationship with your mother in a different light.

Myth	Truth
Autistic people all behave the same way.	Autism is a spectrum and appears in many different ways.

We all probably have a picture in our head when someone says the word "autism." Often, it's based on pop-culture references we've been shown, like Dustin Hoffman's character in *Rain Man* or the character Sheldon Cooper in *The Big Bang Theory* (played by Jim Parsons). Or maybe you picture a person who doesn't speak, doesn't maintain eye contact, rocks their body, and flaps their hands. While these are all real images of autism, they don't accurately reflect the full range of the condition, especially for girls and women, who tend to mask their Autistic traits to socially conform more than boys and men do. As Autistic scholar Stephen Shore famously said decades ago, "If you've met one person with autism, you've met one person with autism." In other words, no two are exactly the same!

Dr. Grandin's Contributions to the Autism Conversation

Dr. Temple Grandin is an Autistic woman who wrote the book *Thinking in Pictures*. Dr. Grandin's story was also turned into a movie, played by the actress Claire Danes in 2010. Her story is that of most Autistic women: She wasn't diagnosed until adulthood. She has been a pioneer in explaining the inner workings of an Autistic brain, and an advocate for better understanding of the gifts and challenges of Autistic individuals within the educational setting. Additionally, she has also been an activist for humane treatment of animals, contributing to the scientific literature and changing farming practices.

Myth	**Truth**
All women with autism are brilliant.	Autistic people have a range of intellectual styles.

Dr. Grandin, along with the character Amy from *The Big Bang Theory*, represents one version of what autism can look like in women. Both of these individuals exist in an academic light, showing a representation of autism that is high achieving and demonstrating "brilliance" in some form. While some Autistic people are incredibly smart, that depiction doesn't represent *all* Autistic women. In fact, when people believe this myth of "brilliance," it can place stress and unrealistic pressure on Autistic women to actually be brilliant. In addition, strong intellectual capability can also present a negative contrast to an Autistic woman's challenges: "Why can my mom memorize three languages and deeply explain the Krebs cycle, but can't consistently show up to my school functions or give me a hug?" This contradiction can be confusing to those around them, and even more confusing to the women themselves. They have often proven themselves academically but find other aspects of life extremely difficult to navigate. It's virtually impossible to sum up a person's intellect in one overly simplistic way.

Updated Media Portrayal of Autism

Thankfully, in the past few years, the media has been focusing on more diversity in Autistic representation, for example on shows like Netflix's *Love on the Spectrum*. This show succeeds in representing the many ways autism presents by having a diverse cast of men, women, nonbinary people, straight and queer people, people from many different racial backgrounds, and all with a range of Autistic presentations. They also have Autistic coaching (an on-camera coach who is Autistic) as well as input on production. As is often said in the Autistic community, there should be "nothing about us without us," which is why having an Autistic voice within these public-facing spaces is critical to educating the world on what autism is and isn't.

Myth	Truth
Most Autistic people are men.	It's about 50/50 in adults without intellectual disability.

Based on current research, the ratio of autism in men to women is at least 2:1 or even closer to 1:1—though the ratio of *diagnosis* in men to women is currently 4:1. As early research was focused on men, the diagnostic criteria are based on the typical presentation of Autistic men, which leads to women often not being diagnosed. Most Autistic women who *do* receive a diagnosis are diagnosed much later in their lives, well into adulthood.

Myth	Truth
Autistic people don't live like the rest of us.	Autistic people live lives just like neurotypical people do.

As clinical scholar Barry Prizant says, being Autistic is just "a different way of being human." But many people don't realize that's true. Autistic people may experience the world in a different way to neurotypical people, but they still have deep and meaningful relationships. They also hold jobs, raise children (like you!), and take care of themselves on a daily basis.

Public Faces of Autism

Some current public representations of Autistic women include environmental activist Greta Thunberg, pop star Sia, artist and actress Tallulah Willis, four-year-old Julia on *Sesame Street*, and musician and actress Courtney Love. Australian comedian Hannah Gadsby, who has a special on Netflix, is also Autistic. Hannah was diagnosed in adulthood, and it helped them understand their anxiety/depression and overall challenges existing in the world. They openly discuss their autism in their stand-up, and share another version of autism that we don't see enough: Hannah highlights that Autistic people can be funny, understand humor, and relate to the human experience just like everyone else.

Myth	Truth
Autistic people aren't capable of deeply caring about others.	Autistic people are loving, caring, and empathetic, but they might show those feelings in nontraditional ways.

This very hurtful myth is simply incorrect, but it persists and it negatively affects how society judges Autistic people—especially if they are parents. Autistic people may not meet neurotypical expectations of emotional expression, but they love just as deeply as anyone else.

Myth	Truth
Autism is a "bad" thing.	Autism is a natural difference.

When I work with families of Autistic children, many people say the day they got their child's diagnosis was the worst day of their lives. They were scared, confused, and overwhelmed. They asked themselves: "Would their child ever be 'normal'? Would they have friends? Would they succeed at school?" These questions were front and center of their minds, because of the narrative that they have historically been told: that Autism is "bad" and Autistic people are "weird." This stigma is often portrayed in the media and through most of our medical and educational systems. But there is a different way of thinking about autism, which is that so many strengths come from diverse ways of existing in the world. For example, being "fixated" on a topic often leads to subject mastery, which can then lead to breakthroughs and innovation, and because Autistic people have unique needs, they're also often more welcoming of others' needs as well. The idea that autism is "bad" is simply based on an outdated way of thinking that says neurodivergent brains are burdensome, when they are actually wonderfully valuable additions to the world.

Key Takeaways

- Autism is a neurological and developmental difference that affects how people interact with others, communicate, experience the world, learn, and behave.
- Due largely to gendered diagnostic criteria and the prevalence of masking, Autistic women are less likely to be diagnosed than men, and are typically diagnosed at a much older age than men.
- Approaching autism with knowledge, support, and accommodations is generally preferred to "treating" it in a way that forces the Autistic person to act neurotypical.
- Harmful myths about autism are pervasive, thanks in great part to older media portrayals. Dismantling these myths can help foster understanding, build positive connections, and reframe negative stereotypes.

Chapter 2

Autistic Women and Mothers

Every Autistic individual is unique, but there are some common threads that unite many Autistic women and mothers. Certain Autistic characteristics can present differently in women, such as the prevalence of masking, the likelihood of anxiety and burnout, and the presence of advanced verbal skills. In addition, some Autistic traits can intersect with the demands of motherhood to create an especially complex scenario for Autistic mothers. For example, parents need strong executive functioning (EF) skills to help plan, schedule, and organize their children's lives—yet Autistic people often need a lot of EF support. Raising small children is especially physically demanding—and an Autistic person's mental and physical energy may drain more quickly in stressful or overstimulating situations. The push-pull of these situations can help explain why your childhood experiences might have felt different from other children's.

In this chapter, we'll try to untangle some of these scenarios so you can better understand why your mom may have approached motherhood the way she did. We'll validate the differences you experienced when you were younger, and look at the ways those differences have carried over into your adult life.

How Autism Presents Differently in Women

As we began to discuss in Chapter 1, autism presents differently in men and women. In general, a lot of these differences come down to the observation that men and boys are more likely to outwardly show their Autistic traits while girls and women tend to internalize them. Of course, generalizations aren't true in *every* case, but that idea can provide a framework for understanding your mother more fully.

Masking/Camouflaging

Research has found that women are very good at "masking" or "camouflaging" in order to fit in with others. Masking is defined as suppressing or inhibiting Autistic traits in order to appear neurotypical. Many

Autistic women say they mask most of the time, but especially within the workplace. Here are some common examples of masking:

- Working really hard to make eye contact when talking with others, even though doing so can be very overwhelming internally.
- Focusing a significant amount of attention to keeping the body still even when an internal persistent need exists to fidget, rock, or move repetitively.
- Attempting to copy neurotypical social behavior like nodding, asking questions, or making certain facial expressions.

If you think about it, neurotypical people also adjust their behavior depending on who they're with. For example, if you're neurotypical, you likely talk to your spouse/partner in very different ways than you talk to your coworker or your boss. You talk to and behave differently with children than adults. You may use a different tone of voice and make different word choices around friends. You might change how close you get to the other person when you speak based on how well you know them. What's a minor behavioral shift for a neurotypical person is multiplied exponentially for an Autistic person because they are trying to exist in a world that was not built for their preferences.

The Goal of Masking

Masking can be a conscious or unconscious process. Either way, the goal is usually to feel more accepted in social situations, "fit in," or avoid stigma. As the word suggests, the person is using a mask to pretend like they are someone else, or attempting to blend in with their surroundings so as not to call attention to themselves. In an effort to avoid judgment for their "Autistic behaviors," they suppress them as best they can. Even though it comes at a physical and mental cost, masking often protects the Autistic person from being treated differently, bullied, or otherwise harmed, and can therefore be an act of self-preservation.

Masking may differ based on culture, but many Autistic women attempt to "fit in" to social contexts more readily than men. Researchers currently believe that women likely mask more than men because they are innately more attuned to social behavior and the cultural expectations of women.

The Negative Impacts of Masking

Masking comes at a great cost to physical and mental well-being. Research with Autistic women specifically tells us that camouflaging/masking is both physically and emotionally exhausting. For example, women find that after masking, they:

- Feel significant stress and anxiety after working hard to "fit in."
- Experience sadness or depression because they are not acting as their true selves. (In extreme cases, this disconnection can lead to suicidality.)
- Suffer from an identity crisis. Revealing your true self in one context, but then not in others, has a negative effect on building and preserving your authentic identity.

Many women have told me that they feel like they never unmask, or only truly unmask with a partner/spouse. Others have been masking throughout their lives and then start to question what's truly themselves and what's their masking behavior. They may ask: "Am I copying others or making my own choices? Am I working really hard to stay focused during conversation or trying to please the other person? Is this my personality or is it being Autistic?" Masking also plays a significant role in Autistic burnout, a topic we'll explore in detail in Chapter 7.

Internalized Stress and Anxiety

Women tend to internalize their stress and dysregulation, while men tend to externalize those feelings. Whereas boys and men are more likely to let that stress out, perhaps through physical behaviors or sounds, women's stress is often more internal and invisible. Women are usually socially conditioned to be quieter, calmer, and more "mature," and many Autistic women sense that standard and hide or ignore their stress rather than addressing it. Masking—which is more prevalent in women, as we've discussed—often leads to anxiety and depression as well.

Repetitive Behaviors

As we've covered, Autistic women tend to internalize their Autistic symptoms, while men tend to externalize. But there are repetitive behaviors Autistic women often do. "Stimming," a physical action that is stimulating, like rocking back and forth or flapping hands, is an example of an external repetitive behavior that helps Autistic people regulate their nervous systems. Many women do "stim," but they also mask more often and more successfully, so they are less likely to display these specific external behaviors. Instead, they tend to turn to other regulating behaviors that may appear more socially acceptable, like using fidget tools, twirling their hair, or playing with jewelry.

Obsessive Interests

Autistic women also tend to have special interests or enthusiasms that are more "socially typical when young," like horses or dolls, where men tend to have more mechanical interests like trains or computer coding. For young Autistic girls, these special interests often align with neurotypical girls' interests, which makes them harder to notice, and therefore identify as different.

What usually eventually stands out is the intensity of these interests. For adults, these interests could be something like animals, languages, literature, the arts, social sciences, or even collecting/nurturing. Often, the interest is focused on observing or thinking about human behavior. In fact, many women share with me that their special interest is autism itself! For women whose autism is not fully supported, getting immersed in their interest is a common way to regulate and find some peace.

How Autism Impacts Mothering

The characteristics of autism are especially complicated when combined with the rigors of motherhood. In this section, we'll begin to connect some of these dots in an effort to provide insight into what your mother's life may be like. Topics like energy levels, sensory sensitivity, and executive functioning skills take on new meaning, emphasis, and importance when considered in terms of the pressures of parenting. We'll go into more detail on these topics and others in Part 2 of this book.

Varying Energy Levels and Physical Demands of Parenthood

Being Autistic in a neurotypical world is, in a word, exhausting. Parenting is also exhausting. Combine the two, and you have a really challenging situation.

For Autistic moms, everyday tasks might require a lot of energy—and a lot of different types of energy—that many people don't fully clock. Managing overwhelming sensory environments (e.g., lights, sounds, movement), changes in routines, and even simple social interactions can demand a lot of physical and cognitive energy from Autistic people and lead to dysregulation. The exhaustion that results can lead Autistic moms to cancel plans, need alone time, nod off, or maybe even appear checked out and uninterested in what others are doing or saying. In some cases, especially when this exhaustion happens chronically over time, it can lead to Autistic shutdown, burnouts, or meltdowns.

You may notice that some of these patterns lessened as your mom aged (though you might notice some in yourself now if you're a parent!). That could be because many Autistic moms have reported that they better understand themselves later in life than they did as younger mothers, and have improved emotional regulation as a result. They can often "know" what they need or what they can't handle once their kids have grown up.

Executive Functioning and the Invisible Labor of Motherhood

Executive functioning (EF) skills are critical for managing everyday life. Think about the daily task of making dinner for a family. You have to figure out what to make, what ingredients you need, when to start cooking, what the steps are, and how long to cook it. If your ability to plan and manage these types of steps is not intact, it can have significant impacts on your daily functioning—and your children's mealtimes.

Even if her children are not young anymore, an Autistic mom may find that EF skills still come into play. Maybe planning social events, family gatherings, or even travel isn't her favorite activity. On the other hand, some mothers notice an improved ability to access EF skills now that they aren't in the depths of managing and caring for young children.

A Mom's Perspective

"While parenting continues to be a challenge for me, a strength of mine is researching. I have been able to find the best information on child development, asses the current trends, and find out what is best for my child. Using my strengths has really helped me feel confident in some areas of parenting."
—Sadie, 35

The EF demands of parenthood are significant—especially for mothers. Parents are required to prepare meals and snacks; schedule the various medical/healthcare appointments; manage cleaning and laundry; plan and coordinate playdates, social experiences, and extracurriculars. Often, mothers who are partnered with men end up doing most of this work, whether they work outside the home or not—in fact, globally, women do about three-quarters of unpaid care work, according to the International Labour Organization figures. We'll talk more about EF and parenting in Chapter 8.

Sensory Overload and Children's Needs

Most Autistic people have sensory sensitivities that affect their daily life. Now think about how much sensory input is involved in parenting children: There are lots of odors. A myriad of textures. Sudden noises. A hundred sensory experiences. While there is more research to be done on Autistic women and motherhood, one study noted that even breastfeeding can present a uniquely challenging sensory experience for Autistic women. Parenting often involves cleaning up one mess only to immediately find another. It can be loud and smelly, and often you have a child attached to you (both literally and figuratively)—which can be challenging to manage even if you process sensory information in a neurotypical way. Ideally, these tasks are divided equally between partners, but often, society expects a woman to be the more hands-on parent in heterosexual partnerships.

Cognitive Stress and Society's Gendered Norms

Most women who are mothers—Autistic or not—likely feel the unrealistic pressures of being a mother at least *sometimes*. You are expected to be unceasingly warm, patient, creative, and loving . . . all while managing a lot of responsibility. Navigating parenthood is a journey that requires a village, as we often hear. What if you have a hard time creating that village, as an Autistic mom might? Or what if the village doesn't really understand the Autistic mother very well? This can lead to a lot of isolation, loneliness, and other big feelings. Your mom may often feel judged by other parents, family members, professionals, and even her own children.

If you are an Autistic woman who is attempting to "act" like a perfect neurotypical mother, it's cognitively very tiring. That means that the brain processing power (cognition) required to act in a way outside your natural style is incredibly draining. Autistic mothers trying to meet modern society's often-unrealistic maternal standards of selflessness, patience, warmth, and endless nurturing can quickly become overwhelmed.

Autistic Communication and Social Expectations of Mothers

Autistic communication has its own unique mannerisms. Whether it's very direct statements, a disinterest in small talk, or a strict adherence to the truth (even if it could hurt someone's feelings), Autistic people often have their own ways of getting their point across. Nonverbal Autistic communication can also look and feel very different from neurotypical styles. For many Autistic people, the nuance of body language and subtle looks isn't easy to read.

All these types of communication come into play while mothering, of course. Giving feedback, providing reassurance, conveying information—mothers of young children do these things all day long. Plus, society often expects mothers to talk in a soft, endearing way, and be very emotionally effusive. Even with adult children, Autistic moms can be direct and show love in a different way than society expects. These demands and expectations for specific communication techniques and approaches can be at odds with an Autistic woman's natural tendencies and preferences.

Looking Back at Your Childhood

Due to the overlapping and often conflicting considerations we've discussed in this chapter, growing up with an Autistic mother often means navigating a childhood shaped by love that may not always have looked like what the world expected. You may have wondered why your mom didn't hug you often, or maybe she hugged you all the time; why she cried easily, or perhaps she never cried at all; why she needed space and silence, or maybe why she was chaotic or emotionally distant at times. In truth, many Autistic mothers are deeply attuned to their children's needs, but they express care in ways that don't always match society's picture of "warmth." For example, their comfort may come through problem-solving, steady routines, or simply being present, rather than through constant verbal and physical reassurance.

For a child, these differences in mothering styles can be confusing and sometimes painful, leading to misunderstandings about whether you were truly seen and understood. If your mother's autism was not well supported during your childhood, your experience might have also been reflective of that situation. And of course, how you were parented as a child impacts you as an adult: This is psychology 101. Your childhood environment—from who your parents are and where you grew up to what your resources were—shapes your future. There are likely both negative and positive, and even neutral, impacts from how your mother parented as an Autistic person.

The rest of this book will help you make sense of these differences—offering a new lens for understanding your childhood and reframing your mother's actions as love that looked different from what you expected.

Building a Unique Partnership As Adults

As you and your mother try to forge an even stronger relationship, there are two core concepts to keep in mind that can help set you up for success: "Both/And" Thinking, and the Double-Empathy Theory. These ideas can provide a solid foundation for specific changes, since they encourage both of you to untangle tricky emotions, empower yourselves, and be authentically you. Let's learn more about each one.

Adopting "Both/And" Thinking

The idea that two contradictory things can be true at the same time may not seem revolutionary, but our minds often don't want to acknowledge that situation. This concept, called "Both/And" Thinking, states that emotions and experiences can't always be neat and tidy—you will run into situations where you have conflicting emotions, or where two people view the same situation with very different eyes. For example, you might love your Autistic mother very much . . . *and* you might feel frustrated at some aspects of your childhood that autism made difficult. Your Autistic mother might love you very much . . . *and* sometimes you might not be receiving that love in the manner you'd like.

Holding two ideas like these at once can help avoid a "one of us must be wrong" judgment call, and instead promote the sense that everyone's emotions and experiences are valid. As you consider the topics in the rest of this book, try to use Both/And Thinking to state your feelings and validate your mother's viewpoint. For example: "I feel like she misunderstands me when I talk about my relationship . . . *and* she's trying her best to give me advice," or "I love our time together . . . *and* I want more independence from her than she wants from me." When you encounter uncomfortable topics, Both/And Thinking can help you and your mother see each other's positions while not judging or critiquing them.

Understanding the Double-Empathy Theory: Take Half the Responsibility

Hand in hand with Both/And Thinking is the Double-Empathy Theory, which was coined in 2012 by Dr. Damian Milton. It essentially states that responsibility for productive communication with an Autistic person is a two-way street. Dr. Milton says miscommunications happen not because the Autistic person or the non-Autistic person is incapable or unempathetic, but rather because the Autistic person and the non-Autistic person aren't speaking the same language. One form of communication isn't "better" than the other; they're simply different. It's the responsibility of *both* parties to make an effort to reach out, learn, and compromise to communicate more effectively. The responsibility does not rest solely on either person to change their behavior, but on both to hear each other out.

Milton came up with this theory after conducting a study using the game known in North America as "Telephone." The game is played by sharing a message from one person to another, down a line of people, by whispering it into your neighbor's ear, until the last person in the line tells the group how they heard the message (and it's often quite different from how it started!). With Milton, the participants tried three lines: one with Autistic people; one with allistic people; and one with a combination of Autistic *and* allistic people. The first two lines had reasonable success, but the third—with the mix of people—struggled the most. That's because the differences in their communication styles seemed to result in a breakdown in communication.

You Can Use the Double-Empathy Theory for Much More Than Communication

Although the Double-Empathy Theory was created in relation to communication skills, the same general principle can also be applied to other areas where you and your mother might see the world differently. If you approach your relationship with her as a two-way street where you can both actively contribute to improvements, you're more likely to find meaningful common ground.

This study helps reframe the mistaken notion that it's the Autistic person's responsibility to fix communication gaps. In reality, it's a two-way street and both you and your mom should be trying to understand each other and respect each other's preferences. The rest of the chapters in this book will provide many specific suggestions and tips for doing that.

Key Takeaways

- Although no two Autistic people are the same, Autistic women do tend to exhibit some qualities that are different from the usual expression of autism in men.
- Autistic women generally show an increased likelihood of burnout, have a greater tendency to mask their Autistic traits, and exhibit different obsessive interests and repetitive behaviors than men do.
- Having autism can affect the way a woman approaches being a mother. Her expressions of love might look different from society's expectations, causing stress and overwhelm for her and her children.
- As mother-child relationships continue into adulthood, new connections—and new complications—can arise. Using the Both/And Thinking and Double-Empathy Theory can reframe those situations in a way that promotes growth instead of further conflict.

Part 2

Exploring a Mother-Child Relationship

Now that you have a solid understanding of autism in general and how it intersects with womanhood and motherhood, it's time to look more closely at your relationship with your mother. All close relationships are made up of moments big and small—special talks, shared experiences, emotional connections, caring touches—that layer on one another to form your connection with another person. For a child and an Autistic mother, the extra layer of autism is present.

The chapters in this part will help you make sense of this additional layer, and acknowledge both the beautiful things your mother's autism brings as well as its challenges. We'll look at a number of key considerations, from social expectations to emotional expressions, so you have a new lens for understanding, accepting, and appreciating your mother. For example, you might share a sad piece of news, but your mother's face might not show the emotion you expect. You might be up for a rigorous hike, but your mother can't seem to muster up that much energy a lot of the time. These disconnects between expectations and reality and neurotypical and Autistic life can lead to misunderstandings, confusion, and pain. They also might have led you to try to "fix" things for her. This part will show you that you can care deeply about your mom without making it your responsibility to make her feel comfortable and happy at every moment. As we examine each topic, we'll focus on both validating your experiences and reframing her actions not as a lack of love, but as love expressed differently.

Chapter 3

A Race with No Winner:

Chasing Society's Expectations of Mothers

Neurotypical life carries both societal and social expectations of how mothers "should" behave—meaning, expectations set by society/culture, and the expectations of people directly around us. All mothers are expected to meet impossibly high standards of care, attention, and selflessness—all while carrying themselves with unending patience and grace. For an Autistic mother, these neurotypical standards might conflict with innate tendencies. As her child, you might have been confused by her approach to social connections—and as an adult, you might still find yourself on a different page than her socially. This chapter will help you:

- **Understand** the social pressures of motherhood.
- **Accept** her boundaries and learn ways to make social experiences more enjoyable for both of you.
- **Appreciate** the challenges your mother faced connecting with neurotypical peers, and how she's handled social situations throughout her life.

Social connection doesn't have to follow traditional societal rules to be meaningful. Looking outside the box can bring you closer to your mother in a mutually agreeable way.

Understand

Managing the Societal Pressures of Motherhood

Despite a movement toward sharing parenting responsibilities more equally, in traditional heterosexual relationships mothers still complete the majority of the work and bear the majority of the expectations as well. According to the Gender Equity Policy Institute, mothers spend twice as much time on childcare and household work as fathers. Mothers are also expected to be the "primary" parent—the one scheduling their child's time, taking them to activities, and handling calls from the school or doctor. Society also holds certain unwritten expectations of "good" mothers that can clash with the needs of Autistic people. Here are some examples:

Societal Expectation	Needs of Autistic Mothers
Mothers should put caring for children ahead of their own physical well-being, needs, and downtime.	Autistic mothers regularly experience extreme fatigue and even burnout, especially from the sensory and cognitive stress of living in a neurotypical world.
Mothers should be emotionally tuned into their children, innately sensing their every emotion.	Autistic mothers might not automatically read emotions in the same way as neurotypical parents.
Mothers should spend more time and energy on their child's hobbies than their own.	Autistic mothers might feel especially deep connections to their own interests, and their hobbies can support their regulation.
Mothers should be able to organize, remember, and plan all aspects of their children's lives.	An Autistic person's executive functioning skills might require extra support.

Trying to meet these unrealistic and potentially unfair expectations on a daily basis is difficult for any mother. But Autistic women face extra hurdles every step of the way.

Constantly comparing yourself to these lofty ideals and finding yourself lacking is very detrimental to your mental well-being. Any mother might start to doubt her skills, lose self-confidence, or feel hopeless. Yet Autistic mothers are asked to soldier on despite existing in a world that's not set up for their needs, preferences, or instincts. This can lead to intense overwhelm, a constant questioning of their own skills, and asking if and how they can do it all. Without much social support or community, which is a challenge many moms (especially Autistic moms) struggle with, your mom may have felt very alone when you were young. Even with some family and friends around to help, many Autistic moms feel unsupported in the ways they truly need help, such as with communication, boundary-setting, and sensory overwhelm.

The Social Challenge of "Mom Groups"

In addition to the societal expectations of being a mom, neurotypical mothers expect a certain amount of social connection with their peers. At their best, these relationships and communities offer a safe place to ask for help, share experiences, get validation, and find support. These groups can be a lifeline for managing the stress that society puts on mothers.

However, it requires emotional effort and social skills to find and connect with communities like that. For an Autistic mom, those relationships might not have come easily—especially depending on her location, generation, and culture. Some Autistic women make friends without any issues, with both other Autistic and neurotypical people. But others may notice their mom didn't have a lot of other "mom friends" that she would spend time with. Your mom may have been perceived by other people in your community as aloof, odd, or maybe cold and unapproachable. But we know from talking to Autistic women that beneath the surface is a person who is capable, empathetic, and deeply loving—these traits are often just expressed in ways that don't align with neurotypical expectations.

For example, Autistic moms might not enjoy small talk or what they find to be inauthentic conversation. They also pride themselves on honesty, and most don't lie—even when it's a small "white lie." This trait can create some tension in social interactions with allistic parents. Your mother may have intentionally avoided shallow mom friendships for these reasons. These fellow mom relationships can also require significant masking, which, as we discussed in Chapter 2, is incredibly taxing and has long-term negative outcomes. On the other hand, not having *any* support groups or friendships at all can add to the challenges of parenting. Clearly, this topic is multilayered and complex.

Blaming Mothers for Autism?

Not only does society have unrealistic expectations of mothers; mothers have even been blamed for the existence of autism in the first place. In the 1960s and 1970s, the term "refrigerator mothering" was hypothesized as to why children were Autistic: It was the "cold" way that mothers engaged with their children that "made" them Autistic. This theory has since been disproven. More recently, the US Food and Drug Administration stated in 2025 that "use of acetaminophen by pregnant women may be associated with an increased risk of neurological conditions such as autism and ADHD in children" (even though it also acknowledged "a causal relationship has not been established and there are contrary studies in the scientific literature"). Both cases seem to unfairly link mothers' behaviors to autism.

When you were a child, your mother's friendships might have impacted your everyday life. If your mom found it hard to connect with others, you might have had fewer playdates than your friends did, or missed some group activities that other moms planned together. You also might have tried to help your mom make those connections. One of the moms I work with shared that her child used to "coach" her on what to do. For example, at the bus stop, he used to say, "Mom, go over there and talk to the other moms." For some children, this can cause a very confusing dynamic of "parenting" their parent. If this was your experience, it makes sense that you may have felt responsible for managing social situations or helping your mom connect. As a child, you were responding to the environment you were in, even if it meant taking on a role that wasn't really yours to carry. As an adult, you have more choice in how much responsibility you are willing to take on in these interactions.

Other Types of Social "Performances"

Being a parent requires being "on" all the time. Parents are required to socialize with others a great deal, like with other parents or kids at playdates, teachers at conferences, doctors at appointments, and people involved in extracurricular activities like sports coaches or music teachers. Given that your mom was likely also already "performing" at work, at family gatherings, and in everyday life, she may have been in a constant state of masking. If that was the case with your mom, you may have experienced her as unavailable, overwhelmed, or easily drained—and it makes sense if that felt confusing, disappointing, or even lonely at times.

For your mom, this constant masking was likely tiring, so she may have needed to recharge at home or isolate herself away from the rest of the family. Potentially, she was less stressed in her own home where the need to perform was reduced, and you may have noted this difference in how she acted at home versus out in public. This may have been quite confusing as a child. You may have been asking yourself questions like, "Why can't my mom be like other moms?" or even "Why can't she just be normal?" Without having the language for it, you likely realized early in your life that your mom didn't act like neurotypical moms. While other moms might have thrived in social situations, your mother might have presented as more of a loner, typically staying to herself or struggling to connect with other moms. That difference may have been confusing or even painful to notice, and it makes sense if you had questions or wished things felt easier.

If this kind of exhaustion from masking happened for your mom, it may have continued into adulthood and it may still be confusing or frustrating to you. After all, social situations don't go away, and her discomfort may influence you to not include your mom in some of your experiences, as you don't want to "manage" her way of socializing. Maybe it's made you question your own social skills and how you engage in the world. In any case, as we will discuss, this isn't your mom having "poor" social skills. Rather, it's that your mom likely has a difference in how she communicates.

A Mom's Perspective

"After social gatherings, I would spend weeks with unexplained stomach pain, never realizing it was my nervous system settling the bill for hours of performing a self that was never entirely real. Researchers found that Autistic brains generate roughly 40 percent more information at rest than neurotypical brains, meaning even in stillness our nervous systems are working overtime. For me that manifests as delayed processing. Fine in the moment, overwhelmed hours later, usually when I am supposed to be winding down. Now add on mom duty to a toddler. When you are still learning to honor your own nervous system while being the calm presence your child needs, those demands compound fast."

—Kate, 49

An important note: Not all Autistic moms find socializing to be difficult or draining; many find community with others—especially other women—who communicate in similar ways to them. I've met several Autistic women who say they have friends they connected with easily, but they didn't know why until later in life when autism in women was more commonly discussed, and they realized their closest friends may be Autistic too. Others even find connections with neurotypical people who innately understand and accept that some women just have different ways of socializing.

Socializing with Your Mother

Social experiences with your mom may have been both positive and negative. From my experiences with Autistic women, when they understand themselves and their needs, they really enjoy time with others. Maybe your mom could plan experiences that suited both her own and your needs, like a trip to the museum, or playing in the park where everyone could have their own space and time. Maybe she was great at organizing activities, like putting together an art table full of creative options you could do with your cousins.

Other experiences may have been more challenging. Maybe going on vacations proved more stressful than enjoyable, as there was a lot to manage from a social, sensory, and organizational standing. Maybe having friends over to your house proved challenging as you didn't understand your mom's behavior and didn't know how to explain it to others. Or maybe your mom masked excessively when others were over, and then was quite exhausted from that effort. My guess is, looking back at your childhood time with your mom, like most children, it's a mixed bag. The hope is that through more understanding, you'll be able to see these experiences with different eyes. Not every experience can be enjoyable for every person, Autistic or not, and that's perfectly okay.

Prompts for Self-Reflection

- What differences do I see in how I like to socialize and how my mom likes to socialize?
- How did I feel about the differences between my mom's social life and that of my friends' moms?
- Have I ever felt like I had to explain my mother's social style to others? How did I feel about doing that?
- Do I notice any differences between how I thought about my mother when I was a child versus how I look at her today?

Prompts for Discussion with Your Mom

- How do you feel about society's expectations of mothers, both when I was younger and now?
- What types of environments and situations do you prefer to socialize in? What sort of people do you like to be around?

Accept

Rightsize Your Role in Your Mother's Social Life

It's important to remember that as a child, it might have been confusing and complicated to try to understand your mother as a social being. It's also important to note that children should not be responsible for making their mom fit into a given social context, explaining her to others, or managing others' discomfort within a social experience. You may have taken on some of these roles as a child, and may benefit from reflecting on what that felt like and what impact that has had on you. As an adult, you have more independence from her as a person, and more choice in saying what might work best for you and your mom now.

If you feel like you still try to take care of her socially, it may help to identify whether this is something she genuinely desires or if it is something you feel anxious about based on your perception of what she "should" be experiencing. Oftentimes, strictly out of love, we can unknowingly try to "fix" any perceived issues with our loved ones, when they're actually content with the life they have built. Try to remember that your mom had a life before you came along, and she likely figured out long ago what works best for her in social settings.

Ideas for Improving Social Experiences with Your Mother

Even if you and your mother have different ideas about what makes for a joyful social experience, you can make an effort to learn more about each other's preferences and brainstorm ways to meet in the middle. The following ideas can help you find common ground.

Collect Information about a Social Event

Whenever you're planning an experience to have with your mother, it's a good idea to get into the habit of considering the social demands ahead of time. Together, you may want to research and discuss some important information, such as the following:

- How far away is the event? How will we get there?
- Will dealing with any logistics like parking or navigating an unfamiliar location present extra challenges?
- How many people will be there?
- How long will we be there?
- What is the sensory environment (noise, lighting, space)?
- What will be expected of us? (For example, will we be passively watching a performance or actively participating in conversations?)

Simply being aware of these factors might help you both better understand what to expect from different environments and therefore what may be challenging about the experience.

It's Okay to Have Mixed Feelings

Given that some of your time with your mother is probably spent within social contexts, you may feel overwhelmed trying to navigate her needs and/or consider her perspective. Know that it is okay to feel both accepting and frustrated with your mother and how she socializes. Remember Both/And Thinking: You may feel some understanding *and* some sadness, or some empathy *and* some anger. These feelings are complicated and valid. There is no "right" way to feel. Seeing your mother's social world through a different lens will take some time and adjustment, so be patient.

Ask Your Mom about Her Preferences

You might start by casually bringing up the event and seeing how your mom responds. For example, you could say something like, "Did you see the town fair is next week?" If she shows interest, you can share more details and get a sense of what feels comfortable for her. As you talk, try to stay open and curious, rather than assuming or pushing—this can help you better understand her preferences and boundaries and keep the process cooperative.

A Child's Perspective

"Once I realized that my mom didn't like being in big groups, but could thrive in very small groups, I realized that I could still enjoy spending time with her and others. I have tried to choose experiences that I know are less stressful for her, which is in turn less stressful for me."
—Sarah, 33

Share Your Requests

You can also be direct in sharing your own needs. You could say something like, "Mom, it's important to me that you come to this dinner with my new partner. You are both important to me and I'd like you to meet them. What plan would be best to make this happen? How can I help you feel comfortable there? Would you prefer it be somewhere quieter?" and so on. Discussing your goals for the event while also asking for her input allows for you both to feel heard and supported.

Make Concessions . . . or Not

If your mother has questions or concerns about the event, consider whether those requests align with your own preferences. Maybe she could wear headphones or earplugs for the outing, find a table in the restaurant that is the most appropriate for her (the best lighting, space away from others, seating that is preferred, etc.), or share how long she'd like to be out. If a compromise works for you as well, great. If not, perhaps she can organize a solution like getting a ride so she can leave earlier, or maybe that particular event is just not a good fit for you to do together. Remember, this kind of issue is not for you to solve alone; Double-Empathy Theory teaches us that it is the work of both parties to find common ground, so you can ask your mom for suggestions that work for her too.

If possible, give both you and your mom time to consider the invitation before deciding. After you've both shared your requests and preferences, let her know that you can both think about it, and you'll check in again the next day to see what you both decided. This takes some pressure off the decision in the moment, and allows you and your mom space to consider what's best.

Think Outside the Box

You don't have to choose only "traditional" social events to connect with your mom. For example, you could spend time together while doing shared interests. If engaging in constant conversation is stressful for your mom, perhaps find an activity that you can do in a parallel way while chatting periodically. Here are some ideas:

- If you both love reading, you could visit a bookstore or library and browse separately for a while, then come together and share what you found.
- If you both love painting, make plans to share space and paint your own pictures while listening to a playlist you both add to.

Connection can also come from consistency and shared routines, perhaps in the form of a weekly stroll or exercise class together. Predictable scheduling can often make both parties feel happy and safe.

When you start to consider nontraditional social events, you'll find that the possibilities and customization options are endless. The important part is that you're connecting in ways that feel enjoyable and authentic to both of you.

A Child's Perspective

"Once I found activities that we both enjoyed, our relationship improved. We happen to love doing word puzzles, so rather than the usual going out to eat, or hanging in big groups within our family, I go to her house and we solve puzzles together. My mom acted so differently in these experiences. It was nice to see how happy she could be around me when she wasn't overly stressed by sounds, lights, and a lack of routine."

—Jared, 48

Appreciate

Reframing Your Mom's Social Preferences in a Positive Light

If your mom isn't comfortable in many social settings, it's important to validate that her social style may have been confusing when you were younger. It may even still feel frustrating today. What's also true is that there are several great lessons anyone can learn from common threads in Autistic socializing. Whether it's the courage to speak the truth or the confidence to be yourself regardless of what others think, you might find she has a rare type of honesty that's actually very admirable.

Valuing Authenticity

Once you think about your mother's social differences through a neurodiversity lens, where you can appreciate how her communication isn't wrong or impaired, but uniquely her, you may be able to more easily respect her way of engaging. For example:

- **Autistic people tend to be refreshingly authentic when they are not masking.** They might not follow the usual social niceties, such as saying what others expect to hear. They often don't feel the need to censor their words and can be strongly rooted in themselves. This sort of authenticity is hard to come by in the neurotypical world, and it can be seen as a real strength when it comes to getting to know who your mom really is. Many people never get to know their parents on that level.
- **They typically won't say something that they don't believe.** Autistic people usually have deep integrity and honesty when it comes to how they communicate, especially in wider social contexts. You likely can trust that what your mom says is truly what she believes, and taking the guesswork out of it means you don't have to decode her beliefs.
- **You likely aren't ever wondering what they are thinking and how they are feeling.** If you ask for their opinion, you shall

receive. Your mom's authentic communication style can make her thoughts and feelings much more apparent to you. While it still can be hard to hear at times, it also can be liberating for you to know how she really feels about situations or people, and that allows her to have more direct and clear connections with you.

Modeling Self-Confidence Instead of Needing Approval

If your mother presents with honesty, authenticity, and integrity, she is modeling a really remarkable way of living. In fact, this way of engaging with the world models a strong sense of self-confidence—the opposite of performing for others. Maybe your mother is never worried about social approval and forges ahead despite what people may think. Many people experience self-doubt and worry about what others think—seeing someone unabashedly being themselves can be a really positive influence.

Spending Your Time Thoughtfully

Because they are often dealing with fatigue, Autistic people may need to focus their time and attention on what's most important to them. Some of us say yes to invitations that we don't actually want to accept, then wonder where all our free time went. What if we dispelled with social niceties and politely declined when that's the best decision for us? Saying no to invitations that aren't right for you is a smart way to make sure that you're being mindful with your time. After feeling upset that your mom did not go to an event, perhaps you can reflect on your own time management priorities and see if there is any room for you to mirror the kinds of boundaries she may seem to set with ease.

Prompts for Self-Reflection

- What positive lessons can I take away from my mother's social style?
- What do I appreciate about my mom's authentic way of communicating?

Key Takeaways

- Social expectations of motherhood often conflict with Autistic ways of communicating and connecting. Behaviors that may look distant or unusual are more accurately signs of overload, exhaustion, or a need to conserve energy—not a lack of love.
- Many challenges arise not from a lack of parenting ability, but from constant pressure to perform and mask, which can lead to isolation, burnout, and a deep need for quiet recovery time.
- Understanding and planning for social demands can reduce stress for both you and your mom, helping you choose environments and experiences that better match each of your sensory and social needs.
- Connection doesn't have to follow traditional social rules—shared activities, routines, and interests can create meaningful closeness without pressure, performance, or constant conversation.
- Your mom's social style may have looked different from what you expected, but it likely was honest and truly authentic to her—which is a goal we can all strive for.

Chapter 4

A Different Way of Showing Love:

Emotional Expression in Autistic Mothers

Mothers, Autistic or not, are looked to for nurturing, protection, and guidance throughout their children's lives. In fact, these qualities of emotional expression are considered the foundation of parenting. You may have wondered why your mom didn't hug you often, or why she seemed quiet or even distant at times. In truth, many Autistic mothers are deeply attuned to their children's needs, but they express care in ways that don't always match society's picture of "warmth." Their comfort may come through problem-solving, steady routines, or simply being present rather than through constant verbal reassurance. Your Autistic mother likely offered these traits in her own way—perhaps structured instead of bubbly, quieter rather than enthusiastic, or more practical than emotional.

While her ways of mothering may not have matched the picture-perfect ideals that society has conditioned us to expect, they were nonetheless expressions of care and love. This chapter will help you:

- **Understand** why your Autistic mother's emotional expression might not follow traditional paths.
- **Accept** that she is showing love in her own way, and learn to ask for what you need in terms of affection.
- **Appreciate** the many ways that your mother's love shines through.

Differences in emotional expression will have shaped your experience and relationship with your mother. Coming to a new understanding about what your mother's love looks like in action can bring you closer together in a way that's comfortable for both of you.

Understand

How Autistic Moms "Read the Room"

A major aspect of parenting is attunement, or the ability to read your child and be emotionally "in sync" with them. When a parent is attuned, they can "read" the needs of their child. When a young child is crying, a parent may know that they are tired or hungry. When a teenager is silent or wants to be alone, a neurotypical mother would "read" that her child is hurting and needs space. Emotional attunement can show up in so many ways in parenthood, and most of us are used to seeing it expressed in neurotypical ways: mothers checking in on their kids frequently, or displaying warmth through facial expressions, hugs, or physical touch. Nowadays, it can even show up as long social media posts, effusively celebrating a child's birthday or accomplishment.

However, for Autistic mothers, it may look different. Your mom may not have provided the exact type of emotional comfort that you were looking for. What likely felt obvious to you might not have seemed that way to your mom, though. For example, you may have thought you made it pretty clear how you felt with your face, your tone, or even your words, while your mother may not have understood these signs—whether the situation happened twenty years ago or last week. If you feel down, stressed, quieter than normal, or short-tempered, you might expect your mom to check in and see how you're doing, but she may not respond in the way you'd hope. She may leave you alone completely, or try to indirectly comfort you through acts of service like folding your clothes or making you food.

It's important to note that research shows Autistic moms can and do tune into their children's emotional needs, but they may attempt to give comfort differently. For example, the emotional expression might be:

- On the quieter side, versus lively or enthusiastic.
- Focused on problem-solving over simply listening.
- Centered around maintaining routines and providing a soothing presence.

- Offering what she sees as comforting words more so than touch.

These examples clearly show love. But if you were hoping for big hugs, vivid facial expressions, and sympathetic commiserating, you might have felt disregarded to some degree. This may have been confusing and potentially upsetting as a child. Maybe you even felt like your mother didn't care about you because she wasn't quick with hugs and kisses. As an adult, you might find that your feelings have evolved, but emotionally connecting with your mother still might not come easily.

Understanding Alexithymia

Alexithymia is characterized by an impaired ability to be aware of, explicitly identify, and describe feelings. Many Autistic people explain the concept of alexithymia as being a contributing factor to their challenges with emotional regulation, emotional understanding, and expression. The word itself comes from the Greek, and means "no words for emotions."

An internal system called interoception often goes hand in hand with alexithymia. Interoception helps us notice and understand what is happening *inside* our bodies—such as hunger, thirst, the need to go to the bathroom—and then respond to those needs. An interoception system that's not as responsive as it could be paired with alexithymia can create a difficult situation where a person's needs are not regularly met.

In your mom, alexithymia may have looked like any of the following:

- Feeling "unwell" but being unable to identify what emotions are at play. (Is this stress? Anger? Frustration? Overwhelm?)
- A lack of awareness of how bodily sensations could actually be responses to anxiety or other emotions (like a racing heart or stomachache before public speaking).
- Struggling to find the emotional vocabulary to describe feelings, sometimes even going mute.
- Not using emotional words to express feelings (e.g., not explicitly saying, "I love you").

Not having the appropriate words to explain how you're feeling can be quite challenging and often has impacts on your relationships. While she may have been blunt with her thoughts and beliefs, maybe you felt like you never knew how your mom was feeling, or how she felt about you, because alexithymia made it difficult to first identify and then find the words to express her emotions. You might have experienced misunderstandings, where both of you assumed the other knew what was happening, but neither one actually did. This dynamic alone can be quite stressful and exhausting, because we all just want to be understood.

Internal versus External Emotional Experiences

Most neurotypical people use nonverbal communication—such as facial expressions and body language—to enhance communication and help people understand their feelings, moods, thoughts, and even perspective. Autistic people, however, can sometimes present as "flat" in terms of their facial expressions. This doesn't mean they aren't feeling many of the same emotions you may be feeling. They just don't express them in the same way because of a difference in brain wiring. How information is processed and integrated in real time can be complicated.

Even knowing that, watching someone *not* show an emotional expression can be quite jarring and unexpected if you've shared something that you're having a strong feeling about. In fact, talking to someone who isn't showing their emotions in the ways that you expect can make you clam up or stop sharing. It may feel like your mother isn't listening or isn't caring, when likely this is simply a misunderstanding: What is happening for her *internally* just isn't matching what she's communicating to you *externally*. Inside, your mother is likely running through feelings of sympathy, empathy, or understanding, but on the outside, her face might seem stoic and still.

Autistic People Don't Lack Empathy

It's a myth that Autistic people don't have the same emotional range as neurotypical people, even if they experience alexithymia. Autistic moms *are* empathetic and caring—in fact, they often have a very strong internal moral code, which can make them active proponents of social justice. So your mom might have been very committed to causes in your community, or she may have strongly advocated within medical or educational settings to make sure you had all that you needed. These are simply different ways of showing empathy than the neurotypical ways of facial expressions, words, or physical touch.

A Mom's Perspective

"I find it difficult to agree that I am perhaps on the Autistic spectrum. Both my husband and I were strictly brought up, which was the common approach by immigrant Jewish parents post-war. As that had been our experience, we did the same for our first two children, although with more expressed love than we had received. By the time the next two children were born, we had definitely softened our approach. At all times, our first concern was that they should feel safe and secure and always be in no doubt that they were loved by us. We found this part very easy. However, I admit I have OCD, and I like everything in order, neat and tidy. It allows me to feel more in control. So it was not so easy for me when any of our children felt extremely angry and refused to 'do as they were told.' I found this frustrating and felt not equipped to deal with the situation gently. Our own parents had dealt with this by punishments and smacking, whereas my husband and I had not agreed with that approach. We tried to be understanding and deal with it more logically, but were not equipped with other methods. I admit now that I sometimes resorted to tears of frustration myself, and acted like they were acting. It shocked them into stopping what they were doing, and in a way that was for me a more positive result. However, now watching my own children deal with their children, I realize there are more gentle ways to have dealt with things."

—Sheila, 78

Sometimes these efforts look "rigid" and "inflexible" to others, as Autistic people might also communicate their thoughts in direct or firm ways. But at the root of these calls for justice, progress, and fairness is a deep desire to care for their loved ones and community at large. Their empathy is present and intact, but the ways it comes out often differ from how neurotypical people show they care.

As with most new parents, many Autistic moms I've spoken with say they were deeply overwhelmed when their kids were young, often admitting that they didn't lead with empathy but with frustration and overwhelm. However, when reflecting on the many ways they strived to give their children a good life, we can often see that their empathy shined through in unexpected ways.

Logical Thinking versus Emotional Responses

Rather than discuss feelings and emotions they may not have the language for, often Autistic people want to get right into problem-solving mode. Once, I was running a support group for Autistic women, compromised of women who had been diagnosed late in life. One of the women told me that she didn't like how my face looked while she was talking to me. I immediately felt defensive, but instead I paused and listened to her explanation of what she meant. She said that my face was showing sadness and concern while she was talking about something challenging in her life. She didn't *want* me to empathize or try to validate her feelings—which are counseling strategies I've learned in my training. Rather than show an emotional response, she wanted me to listen objectively and then offer solutions. She didn't interpret the situation in the same ways that I did. My job, as her clinician, was to meet her where she was and support her in ways that worked best for her.

This story shows someone taking a logical rather than emotional response to problems or conflict, which is a common approach for Autistic people. This can feel jarring at times to a neurotypical person. You might have encountered situations like this with your mother over the years. Maybe you shared something deeply personal and emotional, and your mother's response was blunt and direct, which may have felt unsupportive. Or maybe you vented about a situation, and she immediately began "fixing" the problem, rather than validating your emotions and understanding your perspective. She might have felt that these facts and ideas were protecting and preparing you for future experiences, but they might not have been what you needed in the moment. Regardless of the exact situation, if she offered logical solutions that didn't resonate, the difference in emotional expression preferences could be the root of the misunderstanding.

A Child's Perspective

"My mom seemed to never know what to say or how to comfort me. When I would share that someone had hurt my feelings, her response was always logical, like: 'You shouldn't waste your time with them,' or 'Why do you care what they think?' Practical? Yes. . . . But comforting? No. I needed more. I just wanted a hug like I saw lots of other moms give to their own children. It's taken me years of therapy, and better education around what autism can look like in women, to better understand how my mom was experiencing the problem: as something to solve."
—Luna, 23

Understanding Your Mother's Style of Showing Affection

Your mother may have also displayed physical affection differently than you expected. In neurotypical relationships, affection can look hyperphysical, with big hugs, kisses, picking up, and putting an arm around another person to comfort them. Some Autistic mothers are very physical, while others might show affection through different means, such as:

- Being quietly present for all your activities, but not offering a lot of verbal or physical affirmation.
- Expressing their love through proximity, like sitting near you while you played a game.
- Sharing a common interest, such as enthusiastically researching things you like.

- Respecting your preferences and caring about your desires, like putting all your favorite foods in your school lunch.
- Asking consent before hugging you, or seeming very aware of how touching you could affect you, given their own sensory sensitivities.

Although these forms of affection are not the "typical" shows of physical emotion that society expects of mothers (e.g., warm, expressive, outward), they are equally valid. They may have also showed an understandable uncertainty on your mother's part. For example, if she was silent while you cried, she might have been overwhelmed with emotion and not sure what to say next, so she didn't say anything at all.

Our Story

My mom has never been big on expressing her emotions, and neither am I. My dad left when I was young, so not only was my mom Autistic and undiagnosed with a little kid to care for, but she was also doing it all alone. It often felt like she didn't have time for my emotions, and I didn't see her expressing her own, so I just learned that feelings are felt and not discussed. It's something I'm still unlearning as I enter my forties.

One of my first memories is tripping over my shoelace during sports day at school, and looking up to see my mother's blank expression. She started yelling, "Get up! Go!" but unlike the moms around her, she wasn't looking sad for me. She didn't tilt her head or pout her lips to show she had empathy for my pain. She just expected me to get back on my feet and finish the race. So I did. I dried my tears and sprinted to the finish line. Afterward, I ran over to her wanting a hug and a kiss, even though she rarely did that. She just wiped the mud off my knees, re-tied my shoelace, and told me to go back to my teacher.

I was feeling so much at the time: disappointment, embarrassment, pain. But I felt like she didn't want me to show her those emotions, so we never spoke about it again. Now, as an adult with my own kids, I've learned that most people *do* show emotions through their faces, their words, and their tone of voice. Because most people are neurotypical. I've learned that I can and do naturally do those faces and voices myself, so I've started trying to express myself more.

And, after she told me she was Autistic, I also learned that my mother isn't devoid of those emotions; instead, she shows them through acts of service. She wipes the mud off your knees so you'll be nice and clean. She re-ties your shoelaces so you'll be safe and supported. She'll tell you to rejoin your class and teacher so you won't feel like an embarrassed outsider. She's got emotions—tons of them, in fact. I just had to look a little harder to see how she let them out.

—Dominic, 51

Recognizing a Person's Emotional Availability and Bandwidth

Children of Autistic parents sometimes note that they feel as though their mother wasn't "emotionally available" for them. What does this mean? You might have felt as though she often couldn't relate to your experiences, understand your feelings, or have enough energy to help you manage difficult emotions. This is valid, and likely had a big impact on your childhood.

As we've been discussing, it's less likely that your mother wasn't emotionally available at all, and more likely that she wasn't responding to your emotions in a neurotypical way. Society usually expects mothers to have endless patience with their children's needs, and to put those needs ahead of their own. Autistic mothers might take a different approach. For example, instead of attending your school play (where the sensory environment might have been extremely challenging for her), she might have stayed home but asked you lots of questions about it when you were done. Without a way to understand why, you may have simply felt that something was different about how she handled these situations—and it's natural if that left you with questions or mixed feelings.

In addition, because existing as an Autistic person in a neurotypical world is exhausting, your mother may have been tired from masking and "performing" (as we discussed in Chapter 3). Emotional availability means different things to different people, and is of course dynamic and influenced by specific situations and people. However, with Autistic people, it may feel like you're speaking two different languages, and your version of what it means to be emotionally available might not match your mother's. How her emotions were expressed may not have aligned with your needs, especially when you were a child. Although this difference may not disappear, understanding it can help you approach the relationship differently—finding ways of connecting that feel more clear, intentional, and workable for both of you.

Prompts for Self-Reflection

- What are some ways that my mother showed an emotional connection to me that I might have overlooked?
- Was there a time when I really needed her to speak to me or physically comfort me but she didn't? Knowing what I now know about my own needs and my mother's experiences, how might we communicate about present and future interactions so that we can share a loving relationship together?

Prompts for Discussion with Your Mom

- Between verbal, physical, and action-based styles of emotional expression, which come most naturally to you? Which are more challenging?
- How do you prefer to receive emotional communication from other people?

Accept

Don't Try to Change Your Mother

A key way to support the lines of emotional communication between you and your mom is to bring to mind the reasons behind her style, rather than trying to "fix" her. Historically, Autistic individuals have been told that their emotional style is wrong, and the neurotypical style is correct, and this mindset is quite harmful for them. As discussed in Chapter 1, this treatment-based approach leads to more trauma, masking, and stress for the Autistic person.

Instead, try to lean on the double-empathy mindset and look at the difference in emotional expression as a personality difference that any two people might have. Here's what that shift might look like:

Treatment or Neurotypical Mindset	Double-Empathy Mindset
My mom needs to show more affection when she sees me sad.	I'll ask my mom if she feels okay with giving me a hug. If she doesn't, I'll ask my partner or a close friend for a hug when I need one.
My mom is so selfish. We always have to do things her way, on her time, and following her expectations.	I'm realizing that I need to ask her about her needs *and* express my own so that we can find common ground.
My mother needs to stop trying to fix my problems and instead just listen and comfort me.	My mom is trying to help me by offering all these solutions. Next time I just want comfort, I'll mention that ahead of time so she's clear about the type of support I'm looking for.

Experiment with Different Types of Emotional Communication

Saying I love you, giving a hug, and holding someone's hand are traditional neurotypical ways to express emotions. But they are not the only ones available. Using purely neurotypical styles might not be the best way for the two of you to connect, and could end up being quite limiting. You and your mom can brainstorm (together or separately) other options that could work for you both. Here are some suggestions:

- Verbal expression may not come easily to her. Rather than directly talking, could written communication help? Maybe emailing or texting would work better for you and her. Or perhaps you and your mother could pass a notebook back and forth where you write thoughtful messages to each other. Some people even find being pen pals is a nice way to give each other the time and space to express themselves in writing.
- Sharing images is another way to share emotional connection. You could send memes, photos, or other images that show you're thinking of each other. Sometimes removing language and making everything more visual and less verbal has positive effects on strengthening a bond.
- Oftentimes, Autistic people show emotional expression through acts of service. You might consider offering your help with a task she's working on, or inviting her to help you with something you're doing, like painting a room or setting up a garden. This allows you to show each other that you care through service to one another, which you might both appreciate as a real show of love.

Adjusting your own style of emotional expression can lead to interesting discussions and connections. You might be amazed at the depth of the experience that can occur once someone communicates something in a way that is most effective for them.

A Child's Perspective

"When I was sick, my mom didn't sit on the edge of the bed and stroke my hair or hold me close like my friends' moms did. Instead, she carefully set out a thermometer, measured medicine with precision, and laid out my favorite book, PJs, and blanket. At the time, it felt clinical, even cold. Only later did I realize this was her version of care."

—Derek, 40

Consider the Environment

When thinking about ways to connect emotionally with your mom, setting up the right environment can make all the difference. Sensory processing differences can really have an impact on how well engaged someone is in a conversation (see Chapter 6 for more on sensory differences). Imagine trying to talk with someone at a loud and crowded bar or restaurant. You might be distracted by the noise, your nervous system responds, and it's hard to relax and enjoy your social partner. Now think about this same experience for an Autistic person, from the noise and the fabric of the seats to the tasks of reading body language and facial expressions, inhibiting sensory responses to regulate (e.g., rocking, body movement), and processing tone. . . . These experiences can be quite overwhelming. If you want to foster an emotional conversation with your mom, the setting likely matters.

While you can't always control every aspect of an environment, you may be able to give your mom a heads-up about when you want to have an emotional conversation. Just checking in with her about how she's feeling, what environment she prefers, and how you can help her feel prepared for that conversation can make a huge difference for any emotional discussion. Maybe you can find a quieter place, adjust the lighting, or have a shorter version of the chat if needed.

Accepting the Contradictions

Try to remember that with any kind of connection, especially emotions, two things can be true. Your mother's way of engaging with you emotionally may simultaneously feel unhelpful *and* may be a difference that you can come to accept. It can be difficult *and* loving to do some work on your part to help the situation evolve. The issue likely isn't that she doesn't notice, doesn't understand you, and isn't trying to be supportive. Rather, she's probably experiencing the conversation differently than you, and her response may not be what you expect or need. Remember, Autistic women are generally incredibly empathetic and deeply caring. But the way that they experience emotions internally and express them externally doesn't always align with neurotypical expectations. Know that it's okay to be frustrated by this dynamic, *and* work toward a form of emotional expression where you both feel better understood.

Be Direct about Each Other's Emotional Needs and Experiences

Sharing your needs with your mother can really help your emotional connection. It's important to remember that reading and expressing emotions can be hard in all families, but especially in ones with Autistic family members. Being more intentional with stating how you're feeling and what you need from your mom can go a long way toward building a bridge to a loving emotional connection.

How to Set the Tone for a Conversation

Here are some sample conversation openers that set clear expectations:

- "I just need you to listen to me. I don't need solutions right now."
- "I really need you to help me think of ways to respond to what's bothering me."
- "I really need you just to sit with me and hold my hand while I talk."

Another simple lead-in is "I am hoping to talk about something emotional with you. How are you feeling right now?" It's incredible how just this basic check-in can really shift both party's experiences. I'm confronted with this experience often in groups that I run. When I check in and ask, it's often a completely different emotion, thought, or perspective than what I was expecting. The check-in always leads to better understanding and ultimately a better experience.

All these examples allow you to be direct and clear with your emotional needs and eliminate guesswork. That way, both of you have a better chance of coming away from the experience in a more positive way.

Try to Learn Each Other's Patterns

All families can benefit from identifying each other's moods and physical states before starting an emotional conversation. What does it look like when your mom is well-regulated? Maybe her body is relaxed, her face shows ease, and her tone of voice is calm and measured. What does it look like when your mom is tired or dysregulated? She might immerse herself in a hobby, take time alone in a quiet space, or use fidget tools. If you notice something seems off, you can say, "Mom, I notice you're rocking back and forth a lot. Are you feeling stressed? Overstimulated? Angry about something?" Of course, you can also share your own cues: "Mom, I'm getting a headache and realized I haven't eaten anything today. I'm feeling irritable and need some food." Self-reflecting and then being direct with your mom can help you both be on the same page.

Understanding Each Other Better

In addition to telling your mother that you'd like to speak about something emotional and letting her know what you'd like to get out of the conversation, you can also share your own emotional state in a candid way. Being explicit and direct, again, means that your mother does not have to guess, and allows for clear and honest interactions. Saying something like, "Mom, I'm really frustrated right now. I'm feeling overwhelmed and scared" allows your mom to know your perspective right away. It also takes away the cognitive demands your mother would have to carry in order to read and understand your nonverbal language, the sensory environment, and your words. This integration can be quite demanding and taxing for an Autistic person, both physically and emotionally.

You can also ask open-ended questions of your mom, such as "Mom, when I share something exciting for me and you don't say anything immediately, it feels like you don't care. I'm guessing that you do. Can you tell me what you're thinking and feeling about what I say?" Asking in a curious way shows how you want to accept, learn, and work with your mother's emotional expression style. You could both be making assumptions about the other's feelings, and hearing each other's honest perspectives can improve your connection.

Don't Mistake Silence for Disinterest

Understanding your mother's emotional processing style is important because many Autistic people don't feel the need to immediately fill silences with words. If your mom is being quiet, it's easy to assume she's disinterested or not understanding you—but it's much more likely that her quiet is coming from her own processing or dysregulation. She may be experiencing:

- Sensory overload based on the environment around her.
- A high level of emotional stimulation from the topic being discussed.
- An elevated cognitive demand of absorbing everything you just said.

If that's the case, her quiet isn't a reflection of you or what she thinks of you; it just means she needs some time to process it all. Allowing some peaceful time for her to handle those feelings and regulate herself could invite a thoughtful reply instead of continued silence.

It's important to acknowledge that having this kind of patience with your mom may not be easy for you. In an emotional moment when you are looking to a parent to help, waiting even a few moments for a response can feel like an eternity. It's incredibly hard when emotions are running high to shift completely and feel like you're doing "work" to connect with her when you just need her to comfort you. But patience and understanding really are the key to better relationships and connections. There are some exercises that can help in the moment: like taking some deep breaths to help you get through that frustration. Unclenching your jaw and relaxing your tongue away from the roof of your mouth can signal your body to relax while you await her response. Some people find that after a difficult interaction where emotions are high, journaling can help process the feelings they went through with their mom.

Prompts for Self-Reflection

- How would it feel if I first assume that my mother loves and cares about me?
- What is something I could ask her instead of making assumptions about how she's feeling?

Appreciate

Noticing the Best Parts of Your Mother's Emotional Expression

Now that you may better understand your mother's way of expressing emotions and are working on acceptance of these differences, you may start noticing aspects of her care that you can more readily appreciate. For example, she might have:

- **Unique ways of showing care.** Your mother may not have expressed her emotions in the ways that you may have expected or understood, but she likely was showing that love and care some other way. Try to step back with new eyes and see it, perhaps even list out the ways and return to that list when you need a reminder of how she cares. Maybe she showed love through problem-solving, proximity, research, acts of service, or even giving you space.
- **Deeply empathetic feelings.** Autistic people are deeply feeling and caring. Your mother was likely very committed to justice and fairness, and this may have also influenced how she reacted to experiences in your life that you shared. Add in logical thinking, and she likely was trying to use her emotional responses to protect and prepare you as best she could.
- **An emotional connection that looks different.** Autistic brains are fascinating and complex. Tapping into your mother's "enthusiasm" may open up a new way of connecting and learning about her. Seeing your mother really passionate and engaged in an interest may show you another side of her. You also may be able to find something that you both enjoy that deepens your bond.

Emotional connection with your mother is a critical aspect of a parental relationship, and is often a challenging and maybe even painful area for children of Autistic moms. With careful reflection on your past interactions with your mother, and discussion about how best to handle future interactions, you can invite new and meaningful connections moving forward.

Improved Emotional Awareness in All Areas of Your Life

Working to improve your emotional connection with your Autistic mother will almost certainly pay dividends in your other relationships as well, as you may gain a greater awareness and a deeper appreciation for everyone's differing emotional expression preferences. You'll be able to better understand yourself, and enter an emotional conversation with anyone:

- Bearing in mind that the person's emotional style might not match your own.
- Bringing a curiosity that inspires you to learn about how they prefer to share their emotions (how long they'd like to talk about it, how deeply they'd like to talk about it, how they process and respond to emotional information, etc.).
- Trying to extend the benefit of the doubt that the other person does indeed care.
- Showing more patience, flexibility, and kindness as you go back and forth.

This work also helps you identify, understand, and communicate your own emotions better, which then positively impacts how you engage with others.

Key Takeaways

- Autistic expression of emotions may look different from what you expected, but an Autistic person's emotions are present and real.
- Your mother's expression of emotions can be impacted by sensory experiences, energy levels, and differences in communicating.
- Reflecting on different and unique ways to connect with your mother may allow for a more meaningful relationship. This may include unique ways of communicating your own emotions and needs.
- Consider your mom's special ways of showing emotion as a meaningful context to find connection with her.
- Learning your mother's emotional expression style makes you more aware of others' differences in communication too. You can become more open minded, supportive, and understanding across all relationships in your life.

Chapter 5

Speaking a Unique Language:

Communicating Authentically

A hallmark of autism is a different style of communication. In fact, it's what is often most noticeable to non-Autistic people. People sometimes label this difference in a negative way, like by saying that someone is "quirky," "socially awkward," or "hard to talk to." Communication misunderstandings often come from the fact that Autistic and non-Autistic people are, in a sense, speaking different languages (as discussed in the game of "Telephone" in Chapter 2). Your mom may be very direct when talking with you, even if you were hoping for gentle encouragement or more subtle responses. She may dive deeply into one topic, have trouble changing subjects, or not seem comfortable with small talk. Since communication is a cornerstone of a healthy relationship, it's a good idea to spend some time learning about your mother's style and how to build a bridge to your own.

This chapter will help you:

- **Understand** how and why Autistic people approach communication differently.
- **Accept** your mother's communication style and learn ways to still have productive conversations.
- **Appreciate** the benefits of different styles, like more direct communication.

Even if you two have different approaches to communication, you and your mother can find ways to better acknowledge the other's preferences and aim to compromise so you both get the information, guidance, and respect you deserve.

Understand

What Communication with Your Autistic Mom Might Look Like

There are several common components of Autistic language. Of course, like any other personality trait, these are just frequently observed patterns, and your mother might show one or several of them. Autistic communication falls on a spectrum, so your mom may excel at communicating, or she may struggle significantly, or be anywhere in between. Regardless, learning the background of *why* these communication styles might appeal to your mother can help you see them in a new light.

Direct and Authentic

Autistic people tend to say exactly what is on their mind, and often don't adjust their language and communication style for the situation. This is because Autistic people's brains interpret language literally, and they tend to prioritize clarity and accuracy over social comfort. Due to the way their brains track language and meaning, this approach is often simply the most natural way for them to communicate their thoughts. That means they may say something incredibly candid to you, just as they would to someone who isn't in their family. For example, your mother might not have ever "sugarcoated" anything and spoke very truthfully, regardless of the topic. Maybe she announced that the shirt you are wearing is too tight or your writing assignment wasn't strong. She may not have used softer language when you were younger and instead spoke to you like an adult.

It's easy to mistake this directness for callousness, but that's not usually the case. While working with Autistic women, I have learned how deeply they care about others—it's just that they don't abide by the rules of "social politeness." Even small white lies conflict with their moral code. They are also genuine and authentic to themselves and their beliefs. They tend to speak in a direct way in order to convey how much they care, and not to hurt anyone's feelings. They are prioritizing honesty over society's "hidden rules."

These social politeness rules that neurotypical people typically follow usually don't resonate with Autistic people. As one woman in my group asked me, "Do neurotypical people just lie to each other all day?!" Well . . . yes, actually, sometimes we do! Stop and think about how often you lie to other people on a daily basis, whether to protect their feelings, hide your own struggles, or follow social rules. For example:

- When someone asks, "How are you?" do you say, "Good," even when you aren't?
- If someone wants to know, "Do you like my haircut?" do you say, "Yes!" even if you don't think it suits them?

This conversation style is so ingrained in neurotypical conversation that when someone makes a different choice, it really stands out.

The honesty and authenticity of an Autistic person's direct communication is admirable in many ways. But it can also feel hurtful if you're on the receiving end of it, especially coming from your mother.

Our Story

My mother has always had a very blunt way of putting things. Dad always said it was one of the things he liked about her most. When we'd introduce her to new friends and ask what she thought of them, she'd respond directly, with something like, "They're very loud." Or when we'd get new clothes, she'd tell us, "That color doesn't suit you." Sometimes her way of communicating without any filter could be funny, like when she told our aunt she'd married an idiot. Other times, when it was directed at you, it could be quite hurtful, like when she told me my first tattoo made me look cheap.

When we were very young, my sisters and I would laugh at her comments around the dinner table—we knew what she was saying was taboo, even if she didn't. As teenagers, it was more like an eye roll and some painful internalizing of her words. As adults, we talked about it and decided someone had to intervene. This was just not how people talked to each other, we thought, and we'd had enough. The next time Mom said something offensive, my sister stopped the dinner conversation and told her, "There's a nicer way to put it." To our surprise, Mom's response was "Why would I want to put it more nicely?" That's when it struck me: (a) she didn't understand why speaking honestly would hurt people, and (b) she didn't know why someone might want to adjust their vocabulary to avoid offending another person. These common social rules just did not make any sense to her.

During my first semester at university, I met a girl who spoke similarly to how my mom would speak. One time, when this girl was super blunt, she quickly apologized and told me she was on the spectrum, which meant she didn't think in common verbal communication styles. It clicked that my mom may be the same. I shared this interaction with my sisters in private, and we concluded that because of this and several other factors, maybe Mom was Autistic. We agreed it would be best to read up on how to approach conversations with people on the spectrum, so the Googling began.

Mom disagreed and didn't want to get a diagnosis, so it felt like we were in the dark at first. But it honestly doesn't matter if she is diagnosed or not. Just reading up on how to understand Mom if she *was* Autistic really helped us better see her intentions. We also learned how to discuss with her the impact of her comments on other people without making her defensive. Being on that same page together as a family really took some of the pain away from those awkward everyday conversations.

—Samira, 29

Lack of Small Talk

Many neurotypical people are uncomfortable with silence. When there is silence, they feel compelled to fill it with small talk—meaningless chitchat about the weather, the news, or some other universal topic. This tendency often doesn't make sense to Autistic people. They do not see the purpose in filling that space with conversation they don't genuinely care about.

However, even if they don't understand it, many Autistic people accept that it's a social norm, and they'll at least try to engage in small talk in public situations. That's part of what goes into "masking," which we discussed in Chapters 1 and 2: doing something you don't want to do in order to fit in. When they mask, however, it is both physically and mentally draining. My guess is that this kind of masking didn't occur within your home, so your mother might not have bothered with light chatting and small talk behind closed doors. Instead, she may have been perfectly happy with either sitting in silence or talking deeply about her "special interests."

Specialized Topics of Conversation

The topics Autistic people talk about can also be different from what non-Autistic people tend to talk about. Instead of small talk and light conversation, Autistic people often turn toward their "special interests" or "enthusiasms" as favorite conversation topics. These interests are different for each individual, of course, but there are some popular choices. Common themes for Autistic women include languages, psychology, animals (e.g., horses for many little girls), crafts, history, and art. For many, it's even the topic of autism itself. These topics probably do not look particularly different from neurotypical interests when listed out. What's unique is the intensity of their interests. Their devotion to the interest, the length of time that they can talk about it, and their attention to its details may feel excessive to non-Autistic people. An Autistic person might love to share about their interest but not recognize that they've been focused intently on it for a full hour, or that the other party doesn't share their passion for it and has tried to change the conversation.

Navigating Nonverbal Communication

So much of communication is nonverbal. Neurotypical people usually notice changes in facial expression, tone of voice, body language, and even someone's energy. Sometimes these differences can be quite subtle, but they communicate a lot about how a person is feeling. For example, just the change in tone of voice can completely change a message. Saying, "I'm fine" with a sharp, angry tone means one thing ("I'm *not* fine"), and said in a warm and energetic tone means another ("Everything is really okay"). The words didn't change, but the tone did . . . which completely changed the message.

Autistic people don't always detect the meaning behind changes in tone of voice in the same ways that neurotypical people do, which can lead to misunderstandings. They can miss key pieces of information that their conversational partner is sure they have put across. Sometimes, this can feel like your message is being ignored, when really it just hasn't been deciphered by them at all. Sarcasm may not translate, passive-aggression may go unnoticed, and other tonal patterns may not register. This is often because their brains are focused on understanding the literal words, and less focused on subtle nonverbal cues.

Abrupt Topic Changes

Additionally, Autistic people can change topics abruptly when talking. For example, you might be in a group with your mother, and everyone is discussing a local restaurant. People may be asking questions, listening to responses, and making comments to add to the conversation. All of a sudden, your mother starts talking about a particular insect. You all are confused and trying to find the connection.

Our Story

My mom has long been obsessed with Disney movies, even more than I was as a child. She's always done this thing where you'll say something—anything—and she will reply back with a song lyric or movie quote that it reminds her of. It has nothing to do with whatever you said, but it sparks some kind of connection in her brain and she just has to say it out loud. I could say, "I'm really proud of myself, Mom. I've come so far," and she'd reply with the rest of a lyric from *Aladdin*: "I can't go back to where I used to be!"

When I was younger, it was so embarrassing when she did it around my friends. It also frustrated me because I wanted a real conversation with her, not a rendition of a movie. Now that I'm older and know to expect these responses, I chime in with her as she's saying it. We have a little duet moment. That move has really allowed me to lighten the tone. It makes her smile, like she feels seen, and it makes me feel like I get how she thinks. It's less annoying now, and more sweet.

It's strange, but little changes like that have helped me feel more playful and accepting of my mom's style of communicating. Then I tell her, "Yeah, but seriously . . . I have come a long way, don't you think?" And then she understands that I want a real response. We're both learning.

—Hannah, 33

What is quite interesting is that there is almost always a connection to the original topic—it just isn't always immediately clear to other parties. But if you step into your mother's brain, she knows that this insect is commonly found in South America, the origin of the cuisine you're discussing, and contributes to the locally grown food that the restaurant serves. These types of connections often aren't explained clearly, which can leave conversational partners confused. However, it is just a difference in how individual brains are wired. Neurotypical people shift the conversation with transitional phrases like "speaking of South America," or "sorry to change the subject, but," or "that reminds me." Language like that informs the listener that the topic is shifting. Autistic people learn and store words and concepts differently, and that knowledge can show up quickly in conversation as "changing topics," when really, it is related.

Unique Conversational Exchanges

In neurotypical communication, people usually share the talking time. Conversational partners take turns sharing information, and often follow assumed patterns of asking questions, making comments, pausing, and shifting between speakers. In contrast, Autistic people are more likely to "info dump," which can sound to a neurotypical person like a deluge of information all at one time about one topic. This happens because Autistic people often prioritize information sharing over the back-and-forth style of neurotypical conversation. Sometimes they "info dump" because they're so deeply interested in the topic that it feels almost regulating to let all the information out. It's often a way of sharing their joy with someone they really want to connect with.

Autistic people might also ask questions in a different way than neurotypical people do. For example, they might request really specific details versus general information: Instead of "What did you eat?" or "How was dinner?" they might ask "What was the color of the pasta dish you ate?" which helps them build a clearer picture of the information you're sharing with them.

Other Language Differences

Another area of communication that can be distinctive for Autistic people is paralinguistics. Paralinguistics are vocal differences that are not words, like voice volume, rhythm, stress, intonation, and pitch. Most neurotypical people use these automatically during conversation. These stress patterns and changes in pitch add a lot of emotion to verbal communication, which Autistic people sometimes don't use or read well in others. Maybe your mom struggles to modulate her vocal volume and talks too loudly or too softly during unexpected times. She may even speak without much change in pitch or stress, which makes her speech sound flat or even robotic. This can be because of auditory differences—meaning she may have sensitivities to certain volumes or pitches—or it can be due to the cognitive load it takes to manage things like eye contact, word choice, and physical input all at once. Some Autistic people do use volume, rhythm, and intonation neurotypically, and it may be natural to them, but oftentimes it can be due to masking; they've learned to replicate the patterns of neurotypical speech.

These conversational exchange styles can make a discussion feel uncomfortable if it's not what you were expecting. When you share some topics, your mom might ask a lot of detailed questions—while other topics might not elicit any questions, facial expressions, or comments at all. This discomfort is real, because if you're neurotypical, it's not aligned with *your* preferred communication style. This disconnect boils down to a difference in how you two use language and show your interest. Just being aware this difference exists and recognizing that it's not personal can help you have more comfortable conversations.

Highly Detailed and Accurate

Attention to detail and accuracy can also be an aspect of Autistic communication. Your mother may often question the accuracy of a statement you make, or she may constantly correct your grammar. This can come across as critical, and it's understandable if that has felt frustrating, invalidating, or even hurtful at times. While criticism may not have been her intention, accuracy may have felt especially important to her, particularly if the nuances of social communication felt confusing or uncertain. For example, you may have made an offhand comment like, "We *always* eat there," and your mom chimes in with, "We've only eaten there four times this calendar year." Accuracy can feel really important to Autistic people even while the subtle aspects of social communication can be missed or not attended to.

Why Do These Communication Differences Exist?

These communication differences are thought to be the result of challenges Autistic people often face with integrating the high volume of information they receive in a conversation. If you break it down, talking to someone else requires you to do many things at once:

- Shift your eye gaze to the speaker (or different speakers).
- Read their body language and facial cues.
- Listen and interpret their different tones of voice.
- Process the actual words.
- Form your own thoughts or responses.

. . . And your brain needs to do all that *simultaneously*. Underlying all that incoming information is the sensory experience of the room (how you feel about the noise level, light, physical sensations, and so on).

For Autistic people, this type of interaction requires a lot of integration and energy. They may also need more time than neurotypical people to process all that sensory information and language, and the combination of energy drain and processing time can lead to pausing, delays in responding, highly direct language, and even shutdown or withdrawal from the interaction.

Prompts for Self-Reflection

- How do I best tend to communicate? Am I more comfortable with deep conversation with eye contact, lighter back-and-forth questions, or perhaps writing out my thoughts?
- What about my mom's way of communicating was challenging for me as a child?
- What about my mom's way of communicating is challenging for me now?

Prompts for Discussion with Your Mom

- What part of communicating with others do you find the most difficult?
- What do you wish I understood better about how you experience conversations?

Try Not to Take It Personally

One of the most effective ways to accept your mother's communication style is to try not to internalize it as her judgment of who you are as a person. Instead, know that it's simply her way of conducting conversation. For example, while running a group, I've been told outright that an activity I planned isn't helpful or liked. I've been told that I'm wrong about how I've interpreted an article I've shared, and that they find a topic I've suggested boring and a waste of time. The list goes on and on. Initially, these comments were hard to hear—after all, I had studied these topics and was working hard to brainstorm content for our meetings. However, I've learned to accept this direct style because it is rooted in pure honesty. The following are some statements that show how this tricky dynamic can play out in a conversation:

What Your Mother Said	What You Heard/Felt	What Your Mother May Have Meant/Felt
"That was not when the wedding took place. It was actually in spring 2013."	"She has to correct every single statement I make, and it's about things that don't even matter."	"That fact wasn't accurate and it changes the meaning and experience of what is being shared."
Silence, after you shared that your friend didn't invite you to a party she threw.	"She doesn't understand anything, and she doesn't care about my feelings."	She didn't know what to say, and felt overwhelmed with sadness for you.
She stopped talking for a minute in response to a direct question.	"She doesn't want to tell me what she thinks, and isn't listening to me."	She was overloaded and needed some time to regulate.
"That question doesn't make sense."	"She thinks I'm stupid."	She is confused by the question or the wording and is responding literally.

You Can Be Part of the Solution

As we discussed in Chapter 2, try to remember that the responsibility for successful communication falls on both parties (the Double-Empathy Theory); it's not just on your mom, and it's not just on you. The verbal disconnect between the two of you is a result of a difference in communication styles and needs, not one person's deficiency. Accepting this truth doesn't mean the situation is suddenly easy to manage, but it can make it more tolerable to know that there are not usually any bad intentions, just real difference—and that can open the door for improving your communication moving forward. Adjusting your expectations can also help ease the tension when you're communicating with her. Simply being aware that you will need to be more direct or patient than you would with a neurotypical person can help you set yourself up for success.

Pause and Be Patient

We talked about how Autistic people might need to pause during a conversation to process all the incoming information. You can take a page out of that book and try pausing yourself. If you start to feel awkward, confused, or frustrated, stop talking for a minute and consider what could be happening before you respond. This break can make a huge difference.

Let's say you shared something personal with your mom, but you aren't getting any follow-up questions, comments, or nonverbal language (e.g., nodding, eye contact, change in facial expression) in return. Maybe your thoughts immediately jump to a story that makes you angry, like "she never listens to me," or "she doesn't understand this kind of stuff like other moms do." Stop and ask yourself: "What else could be impacting this interaction? Is she distracted by anything sensory in her environment (e.g., lights, noise, touch)? Did she actually hear me and is just not responding the way I expect? Does she need more time to process what I described?" You can even ask these questions directly to her. Sometimes this pause, and even taking some breaths as you process these thoughts, can allow you space and time to take on her perspective for a moment. In today's fast-paced society, we often expect instant results. Sometimes, good communication takes time. Try to be patient with yourself and your mom.

Also know that it's okay to set boundaries and limits when you're communicating with each other. For example, you can set the tone at the beginning by saying, "Mom, if either of us feels overwhelmed in this chat, we can tell each other that we need to take a break." Or if you're getting frustrated with her info dumping, it's okay to ask her for the "shorter version," or to tell her it's too much information and that you need to take a moment alone. Boundaries are another way to maintain a healthy relationship with each other.

A Child's Perspective

"In the moment, when I immediately don't get the response I'm seeking and I feel annoyed, pausing has really helped me. I spend my energy thinking about what I could do differently or checking in with my mom rather than being frustrated. Of course, this doesn't always work perfectly, but it's really helped my anger toward my mom and allowed me to go to her with questions more often."
—Bethany, 42

Be Direct

You can also try "speaking her language" by being direct and sharing your own experience. This might feel a little unnatural at first, especially if you're not used to that style of communication. Here are some ways to directly explain how you're experiencing a conversation:

- "Mom, it's not clear to me that you're listening or that you heard me."
- "Mom, when you don't say anything, I feel confused and a little hurt. I don't think that's what you intended."
- "Mom, I want to tell you something. Can you tell me what you're thinking or feeling after I tell you?"

You can also directly ask for her feedback about whatever you shared:

- "Did everything I said make sense?"
- "Do you have any thoughts or ideas about what I said?"
- "How do you feel about what I shared?"

Asking clear questions like these can help your mother know what's expected of her, and invites her to give her input.

Check In with Your Mom

You can also check in directly with your mother about *her* experience of the conversation and how it could be better. Here are some questions you could raise:

- "Are you okay if we keep talking about this right now, or is it feeling like too much?"
- "Would it be better for you if I wrote all this down?"
- "Would you rather talk about this at a different time or location?"

"Talking about talking" might seem excessive at first, but putting in a bit of time and effort to meet in the middle with your preferences can help avoid confusion and misunderstandings.

A Child's Perspective

"I'd never really thought about asking my mom what *she* needs when we talk. But after so many conversations where we just didn't get what the other one was saying, it seems so obvious. In fact, we can talk to everyone we're close to about what they need to communicate better. It seems like a simple thing to do to be a better friend, family member, just a better human."

—Peter, 51

Appreciate

See Your Mom's Verbal Communication Style in a New Light

Now that you know more about verbal communication, you might find yourself thinking differently about both your and your mother's experiences with it. When both parties consider it their responsibility to communicate better, you're motivated to share your needs and respect the other person's needs too. With continued experience and an open mind, you'll be able to better understand each other. Of course, this takes time, energy . . . and more time and energy. The goal is making progress in your relationship, rather than feeling like it has to be perfect.

A Child's Perspective

"Trying to get a whole story from my mother is hard. She often shares bits and pieces and doesn't always connect to the 'big picture.' I often need to ask lots of specific questions to fully grasp what she is sharing. While this used to drive me crazy, I now see that this is her way of processing information and I just need to ask what I want to know. We present information differently, and I have stopped trying to change her."

—Will, 50

While verbal communication with your mother still might have its difficulties, the ideas in this chapter should put you two on the road toward more respectful and insightful conversations. You might even come to appreciate some aspects of her communication style, such as:

- **The honesty.** If there is one thing you can be sure of, it's that Autistic communication is genuine. There aren't hidden agendas and you don't have to read between the lines. While accepting this approach can still feel challenging, knowing that the intention is rarely malicious or unkind can certainly help. You may still hear things that feel hard to take and difficult to process, and it's valid to feel that way. You also now know that you too can be direct and clear with how you're feeling and why you're feeling it, and that can help your communication together in the future.

- **There is an opportunity to connect more deeply.** Communication with an Autistic person can be unique. Once you acknowledge that it won't always follow neurotypical rules or expectations, it can be fulfilling. As you embrace your mother's way of communicating, you may "hear" her statements differently and feel able to share things with her more fully. You might be inclined to open up to her more honestly, and you might receive more of her in return.
- **It motivates you to communicate better with other people, as well.** You might find that being direct, honest, and open when communicating with your mother can also work in other areas of your life. Maybe some of the ideas in this chapter could also work with other people in your life (e.g., your own children, a partner, a coworker, neighbors, or in-laws) because those relationships often include communication differences as well.

Remember, communication style mismatches don't mean one person has "bad" communication skills. Listening and engaging with your mother in an open and honest way helps you see that she isn't incapable, unloving, or unskilled at communicating. She is just a human who is experiencing the world slightly differently than you are.

Prompts for Self-Reflection

- Are there any ways that growing up with my mother's communication style may have benefited me? (Am I more accepting of differences in communication? Am I more open minded? Am I more patient than other people I know?)
- Can I think of a recent conversation with my mother that didn't go as well as I would have liked? How could I approach that discussion differently next time?

Key Takeaways

- Communication with an Autistic person may be different from what you expect from neurotypical conversations. The flow, the back-and-forth, and even the topics might not match the way you tend to speak.
- Communication requires a lot of mental and cognitive energy, and that can be especially taxing for Autistic individuals.
- Communication is a two-way street. Both parties should share the responsibility of improving communication. This might mean being more direct; setting boundaries around time, location, and topics; asking questions; and letting your mom know what you want from the conversation.
- There are things you can do to help both your mom and yourself, like pausing, being direct, and checking in with what method of communication works best for each of you.
- The same techniques you can use to improve your communication with your mother can also be used for conversations in other areas of your life.

Chapter 6

An Assault on the Senses:

Discovering Your Mom's Sensory Experience

Most Autistic people process sound, light, and touch differently than neurotypical people, and this can impact how they interact in the world. For example, you may have noticed your mother reacting strongly to certain noises, types of light, clothing textures, potent smells, and specific tastes. However, sensory processing differences go beyond preference, and can impact interactions, relationships, and experiences. It may mean an Autistic person has avoided going to certain places or events, doing certain activities at home, or interacting with certain people if the sensory environment is not compatible with their preferences. Some Autistic women find sensory processing does not make life too difficult, while for others it can be debilitating. If your mom is impacted, her emotional responses to those sensory inputs may also be confusing or unpredictable.

This chapter will provide an overview of the Autistic sensory experience, and help you:

- **Understand** how your mother's nervous system interacts with the sensory world.
- **Accept** that this is a neurological difference, not a choice or part of her personality.
- **Appreciate** the effort and creativity that likely went into your mother's coping strategies.

While your mother's sensory preferences are hers to manage, you taking the time to learn about, accommodate, and respect them can show a compassionate bid for connection that improves your bond.

Understand

Sensory Processing 101

Sensory processing is the brain's response to how our nervous systems receive information from the environment through our senses. We all have nervous systems that include subsystems, which help our bodies take in information from the outside:

- **Vestibular:** The body's balance and movement system (located in the inner ear). It helps the brain understand where the body is in space, and tells us if we are moving, spinning, tilting, or standing still. It helps us keep our balance and coordinate movements.
- **Proprioception:** The sense that tells us where our muscles and joints are and how they are moving without needing to look. It helps us know where our body parts are, how much force to use, and how to move smoothy and safely.
- **Interoception:** The system that helps us notice and understand what is happening *inside* our bodies. It allows us to feel signals like hunger, thirst, the need to go to the bathroom, and when our heart is beating quickly. It helps us recognize our body's internal needs and respond to them.

When the parts of our nervous systems are functioning appropriately, the body registers the stimuli, and the brain assesses the information and responds. For example, if you touch something hot, your body reacts and instinctively moves your hand away from it before you even have time to think. That's our nervous systems at work.

What's Different for Autistic People

Everyone processes sensory input, and everyone has moments where something feels, say, too loud, too cold, or too painful. You've likely also had experiences where you've felt overstimulated or overwhelmed, perhaps by crowds or bright lights. What makes sensory processing different for Autistic people is that these sensory overloads have a significant effect on their daily lives. Autistic people tend to be more "hyposensitive" (have less feeling) or "hypersensitive" (have stronger feeling) to sensory information than neurotypical people. For example, they may not fully register hunger and miss out on feeding their body properly (a hyposensitivity), or they may be unable to concentrate when working near fluorescent lights (a hypersensitivity).

Strong sensory reactions are a component of the diagnosis of autism within the *DSM-5*, under the category of Restricted and Repetitive Behaviors and Interests, which we discussed in Chapter 1. Not *all* Autistic people experience sensory processing differences, but most do.

Sensory Seekers versus Avoiders

There is tremendous variation in sensory reactions and preferences, but in general, the goal of sensory systems is to provide input to the brain so it can "regulate" the body's arousal levels. Arousal levels internally call for either calm or tense feelings based on external inputs from our environment. That can translate to feeling anywhere from sluggish, bored, or tired (low arousal) to excited, overwhelmed, or in a panic (high arousal). Human nervous systems are always gauging these arousal levels, which allow the body to be ready to enact a fight-or-flight response if danger is present. Our nervous systems are constantly trying to get our bodies to stay at a balanced state that is comfortable to maintain. To regulate their nervous systems and keep them in a state that feels balanced, Autistic people are often put into two groups: sensory seeking or sensory avoiding.

- **Sensory seekers invite sensory input.** Some Autistic people seek out sensory experiences to help regulate lower internal arousal levels, like movement, pressure, or sound. For example, you may know young children who enjoy bumping and crashing into things, or feel better after a strong hug. This gives the proprioceptive input to their bodies that helps them ground and regulate themselves. Autistic people may also want to play with fidget toys to regulate, or maybe they really like rocking or pacing. Many sensory seekers also have high pain tolerances.

- **Sensory avoiders prefer to minimize sensory input.** Other Autistic people may prefer to lessen the sensory input in their bodies to help calm their arousal levels. They may choose to only eat a few specific foods, they may have strong feelings about clothing (e.g., they do not like tags or certain fabrics on their skin), or they may wear noise-canceling headphones to reduce auditory input. Certain high-input sensory environments can create anxiety for sensory avoiders, and lowering the lighting or noise level helps their body to regulate to a more comfortable state.

The tricky thing about sensory preferences is that they can fluctuate daily and change over time for some people. An Autistic person may be a sensory seeker in certain environments and a sensory avoider in others. These choices are dynamic and individual, and can take a while for them to assess and learn. As someone loving an Autistic person, what's important for you to know is that managing sensory input could be a 24/7 job for your mother.

A Mom's Perspective

"I can handle exactly two types of sensory stimulation at a time before the feral gremlin within makes an appearance. And, while I've gotten better with awareness and practice, my gremlin is a rage-fueled yeller at heart . . . who may or may not have a history of throwing things. Hot and hungry, fine. Hot, hungry, and in a loud room? Absolutely not. Loud and bustling, fine. Loud, bustling, and tired? Meltdown central. Two children talking to me, fine. Two children talking to me and the house is cluttered? Run. I thought these spontaneous rages were just a part of my charming personality until I had an Autistic child, and the light bulb clicked on. Oh, I'm not a bitch; I'm having a meltdown. Years later, after another neurodivergent child and a lot of trial and error, I've learned that my sensory overwhelm isn't just a problem I have to tolerate. It shapes the whole house. And so, I built a home that works for us. Not for anyone else's idea of what a household should look like. For us."
—Seana, 48

The Sensory Input of Motherhood

Imagine just some of the intense sensory experiences that are part of motherhood:

- **The constant noise.** From the early days of children regulating themselves through crying and toddler tantrums to electronic toys and loud sporting events, there are a lot of noises that come with being a mom. Later, there can be loud arguments, teenagers blasting music, and ongoing noises from video games. In short: Noise is everywhere.
- **The ever-present need to touch.** For babies, nursing, cuddling, and carrying all require a mother's near-constant touch. Even after a child can walk and eat on their own, parenting includes a lot of physical touch like hugs and kisses, brushing hair, and helping at bathtime.
- **A lot of intense smells.** Feeding, diapering, and cleaning up after kids is not an easy endeavor. Once puberty arrives, a whole other variety of smells come into play, such as body odor and sweaty shoes; hairspray and makeup also can contribute to overwhelming smells.

Managing these overwhelming sensory environments takes on a new meaning if you are Autistic, especially if you are sensory avoidant.

Day-to-Day Sensory Responses

Sensory processing differences might shape your mother's daily experiences. As an adult, you might recognize some of the following behaviors as her responses to sensory input. As a child, these reactions were likely not clear to you. This chart outlines common sensory experiences and how they may have influenced your mom's behavior, energy, and relationships.

Sensory System	How It May Have Been Experienced by Your Mom	How This May Look to You
Touch (Tactile Sensitivity)	She has strong feelings about fabrics, clothing tags or seams, makeup, showers, or physical touching.	She avoids hugs, flinches when touched unexpectedly, prefers specific clothes, avoids sitting on certain furniture, or becomes irritable during physical closeness.
Sound (Auditory Sensitivity)	She has difficulty filtering background noise; sudden or loud sounds are overwhelming and exhausting.	She avoids noisy places, becomes tense at loud events, or seems easily startled or "on edge" at sudden sounds.
Visual Sensitivity	Bright or artificial lighting and visually busy environments could cause her discomfort, headaches, or fatigue.	She dims lights, avoids certain stores or events, or seems drained after being out.
Smell & Taste (Olfactory/Gustatory Sensitivity)	She has strong reactions to smells and tastes, even food textures, making certain meals or fragrant environments intolerable.	She cooks a limited range of foods, dislikes certain restaurants, or reacts strongly to scents like candles or perfume.
Body Awareness (Proprioception & Interoception)	Internal signals such as hunger, pain, heat, or fatigue may be harder to notice until they become intense.	She forgets to eat, ignores or misses illness, or suddenly needs to rest or leave without much warning.

Managing Sensory Input Through Routines

Given these challenges, your mother may have spent her life leaning on routines. That's because keeping things as expected allows for control of her environments, and comfort in her body. When you were a child she might have been rigid about what time you ate dinner, who could come over to play, where you sat at a restaurant, and which stores you went to and when. That's because she could account for the noise, touch, tastes, and smells in those familiar places and items. When things go off course, or unexpected plans come up, there is less control and more to manage on the fly, which is harder to handle for neurodivergent brains.

Strict routines can be difficult for some people, especially some kids. You may have found her rhythms and routines to be cumbersome or unnecessary, and it's okay if you still do. Using a new perspective of understanding sensory processing challenges, you may now realize why routines and predictability were likely a huge part of your childhood, and may still be a major part of your mom's life. She has likely been trying to control environments and experiences to avoid since she was young. She probably wanted to be her best self, and enforcing routines is one way for her to exist comfortably in a neurotypical world.

Our Story

I used to sleep in bunkbeds with my little brother when we were very young, and one of my first and most persistent memories of my mom is of her sitting quietly on a chair just inside our bedroom doorway, completely in the dark, apart from the hallway light that shone on her shoes. She sat there every night until we fell asleep. Every single night. It always made me so nervous, like I was taking forever to fall asleep and I worried that she would be mad at me for some reason. I eventually developed awful anxiety around bedtime, and I had terrible insomnia for much of my young adult life. Now that I'm in my thirties, I decided to talk about it with her. When I asked my mom why she used to sit there waiting for us to fall asleep, she told me she was overwhelmed from the noisy, cluttered, socially active day she'd just endured, and her nightly routine to calm down her senses included sitting in dark silence listening to her kids' sleepy deep breaths. It was actually quite sweet.

My mom still hasn't been officially diagnosed as on the spectrum, but she knows herself well. She knows she hates having her hair cut because she doesn't like the sensations. She knows she doesn't do well in loud, brightly lit rooms full of people. She knows she gets burned out just from grocery shopping because of the neon lights and colorful array of options around her. She now understands that as a young mother, her reaction to daily life was that of a neurodivergent woman: someone who had to deal with loud sounds, screams, physical touch, bright lights, and complete exhaustion. On top of it, she was working, raising us, cooking and doing the laundry with a lot of overwhelming smells, meeting with teachers who she couldn't comfortably make eye contact with, and trying to hide all her tiredness because she thought every other woman could handle it so she should be able to as well.

So yeah, it was kind of weird that my mom watched over us as we fell asleep when we were kids. But as an adult, I can totally understand her need to sit in peace at the end of a long day. In retrospect, the fact that she picked our room to do it in so she could enjoy the sounds of us sleeping soundly is actually really touching.

—Gia, 27

Sensory Overload and Its Impact

If she's sensory avoidant, you may have noticed that your mother needed to get back to her own space after a high-sensory experience. That was likely because she was exhausted and her body felt overstimulated. When the body can't process all the input it receives in a comfortable way, it enters sensory overload, which causes Autistic burnout. Signs of this include the following:

- Irritability
- Feeling easily overwhelmed
- Anxiety

- Trouble concentrating
- Feeling emotionally fragile
- Difficulty making decisions
- Wanting to be alone

When it occurs over a long period of time, sensory overload can lead to Autistic burnout, which is discussed in Chapter 7.

These responses aren't a reflection of you, or of your mother's feelings for you, but rather her neurological system responding to overwhelming sensory input the best way it knew how: going somewhere quiet, dark, and alone. The body implements these protective instincts in order to help the person regulate their nervous system and bring it back to a balanced state.

Masking and Regulation

When experiencing overwhelming sensory experiences, Autistic women are more likely than men to suppress the visible signs of their discomfort, so that they appear "normal" or meet social expectations—in other words, they mask. Your mother may have appeared "fine" in public because she was masking, but then she unmasked or shut down later when she was in a place where she felt safe. Since this place was likely your home, it might have seemed like she *wasn't* comfortable at home, trying to be alone and in silence, when in fact it was the opposite. Home might have been the only place she felt able to recover from the sensory overload caused by the outside world.

Prompts for Self-Reflection

- How do I feel in my body in different situations like noisy or hot spaces?
- How do I deal with feelings of overwhelm or understimulation?

Prompts for Discussion with Your Mom

- Which parts of motherhood are most challenging for you from a sensory standpoint?
- How can I help you feel more comfortable when these situations come up in the future?

Accept

Acknowledge Any Feelings of Rejection and Abandonment

Growing up with a mother with sensory processing differences likely had significant impacts on your childhood experiences. If she tends to be sensory avoidant, you may have felt like your mom was rejecting or abandoning you if she resisted touch, shut out noise, or needed time alone. In reality, she was avoiding a sensory experience and likely seeking time and space to regulate her nervous system. If she tends to be sensory seeking, you may have felt like she was constantly trying to hug you when you didn't want it, or like she always had loud noises on around her that may have felt chaotic and like you were being ignored. Over time, this kind of mismatch can leave you feeling disconnected or uncertain, and it's valid if that shaped how you experienced your relationship with her. Try to remember these behaviors aren't meant to show disinterest in you; rather, they are a coping mechanism used to allow her body to comfortably process sensory information.

Depending on your mother's awareness of autism, it's possible that she didn't even understand her own sensory system, let alone be able to explain it to others. She probably hasn't had language to describe her experiences, she may not have had support from others to best learn and understand her system, and she's likely had no sense of an Autistic community that could validate what she's been going through. Even today, she might not have these options.

When reflecting on your relationship with your mom through a sensory lens, it's important to acknowledge that any challenges she experienced when you were young weren't solely a result of parenting; they have always existed due to her autism. Still, your mom's sensory overload could have resulted in having many of your childhood needs unmet, and it's important to acknowledge how difficult that situation was and may even continue to be. It may be healing to discuss with her how you interpreted and experienced different situations when you were young. You could consider saying something like, "I'm realizing now that sensory experiences were and likely still are challenging for you. For me, when you avoided noise from the TV, it felt like you didn't want to hang out with me. What was it like for you? Can you see how I experienced it?"

The hope is that you will at some point be able to look back on your childhood experiences with different, maybe gentler, eyes. This kindness should apply to what both you and your mother have gone through, from your early childhood all the way up to the present day.

A Child's Perspective

"I remember always thinking my mother overreacted to small things. She hated crowded stores or events, got irritable during long family gatherings, and often needed to leave things early. At home, she seemed completely depleted by the end of the day. We'd often see her sitting silently in dim rooms while the rest of us continued talking around her. I interpreted this as disinterest or emotional distance. Years later, after my mother began learning about autism in women, things started to make more sense. She described living in a constant state of sensory strain without realizing it had a name. She had spent decades pushing through discomfort because she believed everyone felt that way. It felt like she was avoiding us, but now I understand it more as survival."
—Olivia, 44

Talk Through Her Current Sensory Needs

Sensory systems are layered, complicated, and can change over time, so what was true about your mother's sensory preferences when you were young might not match what they are now. To try to understand her better, you could ask if she is open to discussing them with you. An honest conversation can give you insight into her sensory life and perhaps give you an opportunity to share your side of those experiences with her. Both of you feeling heard can be very validating.

Here are some open-ended questions to ask that lead with curiosity and can invite your mom to share honest information and feelings:

- "What physical environments are the hardest for you?"
- "What does it feel like in your body when your senses are overloaded?"
- "What environments make you feel the most like yourself? The safest?"
- "Are there things I can do to help you when you feel upset or uncomfortable with a sensory situation?"
- "How can I tell that you are feeling dysregulated because of sensory input?"
- "Is there anything you wish I knew about how the outside world feels to you?"

While you are not responsible for ensuring that your mother's sensory environment is always perfect, knowing the answers to these questions can give you great insight into her experience and allow you to proceed without as much guessing or uncertainty. Maybe you've spent time trying to figure out why she is acting a certain way, asking yourself, "Was it something I did or said?" or "Why isn't she enjoying time with me?" These kinds of questions are full of self-doubt; they take away from your own enjoyment and from your relationship. Getting clear answers can help. If you can talk through things honestly, you may also be able to create more environments that work for you both.

Hearing about how your mom experiences the sensory world may help you better grasp who she is, what makes her happy or sad, and how she acts when she feels uncomfortable. It may also help you to understand that some previous assumptions you held could have been wrong. For example, maybe you felt she was being distant from you when she was really overwhelmed by sounds. Or maybe she seemed irritable in bright rooms, but it was nothing to do with anything you did. Anger and resentment can linger from the stories we tell ourselves, and seeing those stories through clearer eyes can help you understand yourself better, let those stories go, and more clearly understand the other person's actions. Even if you can't, you will be able to understand that her sensory experiences aren't a choice, and her behaviors don't necessarily mean that she doesn't want to be with you.

Help with Sensory Input of Grandchildren

If you have your own children or nieces and nephews, you might be considering the sensory environment that they create for your mom. Your mother might have gotten to know herself well enough to set the kinds of boundaries that help her feel regulated, or she may be looking forward to a positive grandparent relationship but needs support with the sensory challenges.

As we discussed earlier, children bring a lot of joy to the table—and a lot of noise, touch, and smells as well. They are often unpredictable, and while their happiness can be infectious, they also can make socializing, traveling, and engaging with others more complicated. It may also bring up your past childhood experiences for you when you see your mother's reactions to your own children's or your sibling's children's behavior.

Many older Autistic moms say they've grow into more regulated Autistic grandmothers. So even if your mom struggled with sensory input when you were young, the next generation may not be as impactful. If she does struggle with kids in your family, like perhaps she needs to leave the room when they make noise or she gets upset when they run into her, it's important to consider what may underlie these reactions. Could this sensory environment be negatively impacting your mom? Is it just too loud and chaotic? Or are you worried her reactions may be upsetting the children? It is important for parents to honor their own needs and model that self-advocacy to their children, and it's especially important that it is not the responsibility of the child to figure that out. What's most important is to try and understand these situations and discuss them with your mother, especially if she's trying to form a bond with your kids. Here are some questions that can help you identify potential issues ahead of time:

- "When is the best time for the kids to visit you?" (e.g., mornings, afternoons, weekends)
- "If we come and stay at your house, do any specific circumstances make it hard?"
- "Are there things that I can do to make the visit easier?"
- "Are there preferred places we can go together?"

- "Which activities do you enjoy doing with your grandchildren?"
- "Is it best if we get a hotel and stay nearby instead of in your home?"

Working out some of these details in advance can help everyone focus on the joys of a grandparent-grandchild relationship.

A Mom's Perspective

"I wish when I was raising my children that I had been more direct with them about my needs. I wish I had said, 'Mom's brain is really tired from the day; I just need fifteen minutes in my room alone to give it a rest. Then let's play our card game.' Or 'When we go grocery shopping, I'm going to wear these cool headphones. They help me stay focused and less overwhelmed. Then we can be done and home!' I think being direct and clear would have been beneficial to us both. I would have felt less guilty and overwhelmed, and my children would have better understood me."

—Joann, 65

Appreciate

Admiring Resilience

Looking back on your childhood through a lens that recognizes sensory processing differences, you may be able to see just how resilient your mother is. While navigating motherhood, which itself comes with a lot of stress and challenge, your mother was also trying to cope with an Autistic sensory system that may have made parenting even harder.

Whether it was done consciously or not, your mother likely developed several different strategies that she used to address sensory overwhelm so she could still show up for you whenever possible. Things like routines and predictability likely allowed her to be as present and engaged in her parenting as she could be.

A Child's Perspective

"I didn't have words for it then, and I don't think my mom did either, but she was teaching me about sensory needs from a young age. When she was telling me to turn certain lights off in the evening, she was not just being picky; she was responding to what her body was telling her it needed. When she was asking me to turn down the volume on my video games, she wasn't just being grumpy with me; she was showing me that a loud environment really raised her stress levels. She was unknowingly teaching me something about communication and self-care."

—Elijah, 30

A Focus on Self-Care

Self-care is about figuring out what you need to feel better, and communicating it to the world. Your mom may have learned to advocate for herself in that kind of direct way, telling people around her that she needed time and space when she felt overstimulated. If she did this, she modeled for you how to set boundaries and listen to your body. She taught you not only to take care of yourself, but also to be clear and honest with others about your needs, which is a strong self-care skill that many of us aim to develop.

If she wasn't able to advocate for herself and she instead muddled through the day overwhelmed, she likely took the time she needed to regulate herself once she got to a safe space like home. Even if it was delayed, this may have showed you that rest is highly important. Many of us could use more practice in identifying and responding to our internal needs, so if you gained this skill from your mother, that is truly something to be grateful for.

Promoting an Awareness of Sensory Issues

Now that you've learned about sensory processing, you can bring that knowledge into both your relationship with your mother and areas of your life beyond. You may have your own sensory sensitivities and can now better understand yourself and how those sensitivities affect your life. You might recognize sensory processing differences in others, perhaps in other family members too, and you can be ready to support and compromise with anyone who prefers a quiet room or a fidget tool.

Simply being aware that not everyone processes sensory input in the same way can encourage you to treat others with more grace and compassion than you might have previously. Society often teaches us to negatively judge many Autistic behaviors or habits, but knowing that they could be nervous system responses allows you to see them in a very different light.

Prompts for Self-Reflection

- How has my mother helped me listen to my own body?
- What will I do differently now that I know more about sensory processing differences?

Key Takeaways

- Sensory processing differences are neurological, often invisible, and deeply shape how Autistic people experience everyday life. These differences can affect comfort, energy, behavior, and emotional regulation in ways that children can easily misunderstand.
- Many of your mother's reactions, routines, withdrawals, or irritable moments may have come from sensory overload and the effort of masking—but that doesn't mean they didn't affect you or the way you experienced your relationship with her. This understanding isn't about excusing what happened, but about giving you a fuller picture as you make sense of your experiences. You can hold both truths at once: Her behavior may have had underlying reasons, and it still affected you in meaningful ways.
- Your mother's sensory challenges existed long before your childhood and were not a reflection of rejection, but of a nervous system coping without understanding, language, or adequate support.
- Accepting this experience means holding two truths at once: acknowledging the impact of your unmet needs while recognizing that routines, avoidance, and rigidity were likely protective strategies for your mom.
- Seen through a sensory lens, your mother's routines, planning, and boundaries reflect resilience. These were quiet strategies that allowed her to show up, care deeply, and model self-awareness, preparation, and respect for limits that you may now carry into your own life.

Chapter 7

Running on Empty:

Understanding Your Mom's Energy Levels

Parenting is an exhausting endeavor. Parenting with autism is especially tiring. You might notice that when you were young your mom was frequently tired or withdrawn, or that even now you've grown up she might show inconsistent energy levels. Perhaps there are moments when she is deeply engaged and capable, followed by periods when she needs to retreat, rest, or disengage entirely. This chapter will help explain how energy functions within an Autistic nervous system so you have a stronger frame of reference for how your mom might operate.

This chapter will teach you about the different types of energy we use every day, and:

- **Understand** concepts such as Autistic burnout and the Spoon Theory, and how they affect your mother's energy levels.
- **Accept** that your mother's energy levels may be uneven, fragile, or unpredictable—even when her intentions are good.
- **Appreciate** that everyone's energy levels fluctuate to some degree.

These frameworks do not erase the impact of your experience, nor do they ask you to rewrite your past. Instead, they offer context and language that many children of Autistic women did not have during their childhood. Understanding how energy is spent, depleted, and managed can help clarify behaviors that previously felt personal or confusing, and can open space for a more accurate, compassionate connection that allows for your mother's energy needs.

Understand

Using Spoon Theory to Understand Autistic Energy Usage

Spoon Theory is a way to visualize energy use that originated in the chronic illness community. It comes from chronic illness advocate Christine Miserandino, who, in 2003, was trying to explain energy levels to her friend at a diner, and she grabbed some spoons to represent energy levels and needs.

What Is Spoon Theory?

Spoon Theory essentially states that while most neurotypical people have unlimited "spoons" (internal energy) to get through the day, those with chronic illness and neurodiversity only have a set number of spoons. Neurotypical people can much more easily go back to the drawer and grab another spoon when they need one. But it doesn't work that way for Autistic people.

For example, let's say an Autistic mom has ten spoons to start her day, signifying ten units of her own energy. Each task she will take on that day requires a certain number of spoons. Let's say getting dressed costs two spoons, driving to work costs another two spoons, work tasks use up three more spoons, and so forth. Certain tasks usually "cost" a lot of spoons for Autistic people, such as:

- Managing sensory environments, such as loud noises, uncomfortable clothing, or overwhelming odors.
- Shifting between tasks, making decisions, and problem-solving.
- Interacting socially, including managing eye contact, generating topics for conversation, "masking" Autistic behavior, interpreting body language, and interpreting tone of voice.

When an Autistic person is out of spoons, they are out of spoons—going to get more from the drawer isn't an option—and they're left too tired and drained to do anything more.

There is some nuance in Spoon Theory:

- People may wake up with a different number of spoons each day.
- Spoons can represent different types of energy as well. A person may have a lot of spoons available for, say, mental focus, but very few spoons available for social tasks.
- Spoons can be used up unexpectedly due to sensory overload or an unplanned change in their day.
- Certain habits—such as resting, regulating sensory inputs, or participating in enjoyable hobbies—can add to or replenish spoon totals.

You can imagine, for Autistic people, how difficult it is to plan your spoon uses as your priorities and needs change constantly over the course of a day.

Parenting and the Spoon Theory

Understanding the Spoon Theory can help you visualize your mother's energy levels and capacity. Parenting, at baseline, requires excessive amounts of energy. Most parents will tell you that they are exhausted and overwhelmed by the ongoing demands of raising children. Autistic mothers are managing those same duties along with a different energy system at baseline.

With this concept in mind, think about the endless tasks that your mother did for you and your family, and how many spoons it may have cost for her to do them. This mindset may help you understand why some situations occur. For example:

- Maybe your mom's intention was to go to your school event at the end of the day, but her plans changed and by then her spoons were all used up.
- Maybe your mom leaves events or engagements before they end because she ran out of spoons by focusing on conversations and engaging under bright lights.

- She may also not even attempt to plan events or do certain tasks because she already knows that they require more spoons than she typically has.
- Maybe you've seen her thriving and energetic when it comes to a special interest or engaging in tasks that regulate her nervous system, showing how she can replenish her spoon supply.

The ebb and flow of your mother's energy levels can be confusing to witness, both when you were a child and now as an adult. You might see her have a lot of energy for certain things, and then nothing for others. The Spoon Theory can help you understand that different events likely required a different numbers of spoons, and your mom was managing her energy levels as best she could.

What Is Autistic Burnout?

Whether or not we are neurodivergent, when our energy levels aren't properly managed, it can result in burnout. When most people think about the term "burnout," they think of it in neurotypical terms, which means feeling drained from a specific short-term stress, like an especially busy time at work or with caretaking. You may get burned out from intense deadlines, a huge workload, or the stress of arguing with a loved one. However, Autistic burnout causes a serious nervous system response that comes from chronically adapting to a world not built for you. Sensory overload, constant masking, and social processing can drain energy daily. Neurotypical burnout can usually be repaired with brief rest, but Autistic burnout, on the other hand, has been built up chronically over years and can be extremely hard to manage.

Signs and Symptoms

Autistic burnout is an intense level of exhaustion and shutdown that occurs over time. It builds over a lifetime of adaption, of living in a mainly neurotypical world and attempting to function in it. The degree of Autistic burnout might also wax and wane depending on the person's life circumstances. Common signs of Autistic burnout include the following:

- Decrease in or loss of the ability to talk (mutism).
- Decrease in or loss of executive functioning skills (inability to focus, brain fog, task completion issues).
- Decrease in or loss of ability to regulate emotions (easily crying, breaking down, becoming numb).
- Increase in sensory sensitivity (being even more easily impacted by light, sound, smell, and touch).
- Increase in feelings of overwhelm, even with basic tasks like hygiene or making meals.
- Increase in needed alone time.

As a child, if you saw your mom experiencing Autistic burnout from everyday things, you might have tried to make sense of these responses by assuming it was your behavior or needs that were bothering her. Many adult children recall wondering whether they were asking for too much, whether their needs were burdensome, or whether their mother's exhaustion meant something about her interest, care, or love for them. But the truth is that Autistic burnout is most often caused by other factors than just parenting; it's a long-term mismatch between her body and its environment.

A Mom's Perspective

"Some days, just showing up for my children would use every ounce of energy that I have. I'm trying to balance their needs with my own . . . and I don't always understand or know what I need to make that easier."
—Marianne, 54

Common Causes of Autistic Burnout

Every individual who experiences Autistic burnout will have their own combination of triggers, but there are common threads as well.

Masking

As we discussed in Chapter 2, Autistic women are more likely to mask and camouflage their Autistic behaviors while copying neurotypical behaviors in order to fit in with neurotypical people around them. Masking drains a lot of energy, both physical and cognitive. Burnout can result when the body is devoting so many resources to inhibiting one set of behaviors and unnaturally promoting another.

It takes a lot of cognitive effort to crack the code and to constantly try and keep up with neurotypical conversations and interactions when it doesn't come naturally. There is also a level of inhibiting physical Autistic behaviors. For example, an Autistic person might regulate their emotions by rocking their body slightly back and forth or moving their hands quickly (known as "stimming," as discussed in Chapter 2). However, your mother may have known that this would be seen as "odd" to do in a neurotypical setting, so she likely worked hard *not* to do this, and that tamping down comes at a cost. This nonstop experience of trying to be who you are not is draining, which is why it contributes so much to Autistic burnout.

Managing Sensory Input

Constantly managing sensory environments that don't align with how you process sound, touch, space, or light also contributes to Autistic burnout. We've all had those feelings of being overstimulated. Maybe you're at a store and it's loud and bright and overcrowded—and you're with someone who you're trying to converse with. It can feel overwhelming and you feel such relief and exhaustion when you get to your car, alone. Imagine this experience almost *all the time*. This kind of experience can be a constant state for an Autistic person in a neurotypical world. Their bodies process all the sensory input differently, and it's exhausting navigating it all constantly.

Unrealistic Expectations

Autistic burnout can also come from being worn down by society's unrealistic expectations, especially of women, and especially of mothers. Society expects mothers to have a career, engage with the community, participate in school functions, prepare meals, maintain a social life, raise their kids, often care for their parents, and organize their family—all of which requires an inordinate amount of time, energy, focus, executive functioning skills, and selflessness. There is no "rest" from this way of life. This is often the reason that your mother may have appeared exhausted, withdrawn, or even avoidant. It wasn't that your needs were "too much"; it's that society was asking too much of her.

Managing Autistic Burnout

Neurotypical women typically cope with their own burnout by setting boundaries and focusing on rest and sleep. They also learn to figure out what "fuels" them, which could be seeing close friends or doing their own hobbies, for example. These same coping strategies may not be what works for your mom, though. She may simply need time, space, and silence in larger quantities than neurotypical moms do.

Your mother likely didn't know during your childhood what Autistic burnout was. (Maybe she still doesn't!) She also might not realize how much energy it takes to "fit in" or conform to neurotypical expectations. These concepts are all somewhat new, even to some members of the Autistic community.

A Child's Perspective

"Hearing my mom talk about things she loved was when I saw how happy it made her. It was often a lot to listen to, and I often didn't want to listen. I didn't understand why it would take over her time . . . but now understand that it was regulating and really an expression of who she was. It continues to bring her joy."

—Deb, 46

Shutdowns and Meltdowns

Now that we've learned about Autistic burnout, it's important to also know about shutdowns and meltdowns. When they are overloaded in terms of emotions or sensory experiences, Autistic people can experience shutdowns and meltdowns fairly quickly.

- Autistic **meltdowns** can manifest as somewhat outward and explosive, for example crying or yelling, lashing out, pacing, or aggression toward themselves or others.
- **Shutdowns** tend to be more internal responses, more like silence and stillness, or difficulty speaking or moving.

Our Story

I remember thinking it was strange how my mother could look so capable in some contexts, but so drained in others. At a school fundraiser, she stood near the folding tables and smiled at the other parents. She asked the right questions. She laughed at the right moments. However, when I watched her closely, I saw that she stood alone and only moved when she had to. At the time, I thought she was shy. Or aloof. Or weird. Or simply uninterested.

On the drive home, she was quiet. By the time we pulled into the driveway, she said she had a headache. Once inside, she went straight to her bedroom and closed the door. No debrief. No rehashing the night. No "Wasn't that nice?" the way other parents seemed to do. As a child, I filled in the gaps myself and assumed that she didn't like being at school events. Or I did something wrong. I wasn't interesting enough to talk to.

Years later, I understand something I couldn't then. The version of my mother I saw in public took so much out of her. How she was acting took a lot of effort, and what looked like distance afterward was actually depletion. She had spent the evening gauging people's facial expressions, expectations, timing, and conversation, and holding herself together. By the time we got home, there was nothing left to offer—not because she didn't care, but because she had already given it all.

—Leah, 56

Both shutdowns and meltdowns are a result of overwhelm from the environment, or the demands of the situation. A meltdown can also lead to a shutdown, so an outburst of aggression or crying heavily can lead to an Autistic person going silent and still. In both cases, it's important to know that these aren't like childhood tantrums, which can be behaviors that are trying to manipulate outcomes. Rather, this is an involuntary nervous system response to an external situation.

For example, when navigating a disagreement between you and your sibling, your mother could have felt incredibly overwhelmed with the sounds of arguing and she may have had a meltdown, which could have looked like crying or intense emotions directed at you or to herself. On the other hand, your mother may have responded with a shutdown, where she tended to have an internal experience. This may have looked like freezing, becoming nonverbal, or even withdrawing completely. Both are responses to overwhelm.

It's important to note that it might have been concerning, confusing, painful, or even scary for you as a kid to have witnessed your mom having meltdowns or shutdowns. It may have even resulted in aggression toward you as a child, which is never acceptable. Learning that these behaviors may have happened in relation to autism may bring you more understanding, but it doesn't take away how it affected you. If your experience with these situations was painful, I invite you to pause with that feeling now, without explaining away the impact with reasons. Consider whether it may help you to write about your memories and feelings, talk to a trusted loved one, or process these emotions in either individual or family therapy.

Energy Boosts

There is no one single "fix" for burnout, shutdowns, or meltdowns. But, like all people, after rest and time, Autistic women can find activities and experiences that support and replenish their energy reserves. Many Autistic people find that engaging with their special interests or enthusiasms boosts their energy levels. For example, maybe your mother loves learning about languages, and using an app to practice vocabulary gives her joy. Or maybe she loves playing strategy games in person or online. Other people like engaging in hobbies that involve artistic creation, like pottery or knitting.

The possibilities are endless and unique to your mom. It could be helpful for you to understand these enthusiasms and know how meaningful and important they are not only to your mom's joy but also to her energy levels.

Prompts for Self-Reflection

- What drains or boosts my energy levels?
- In what ways did my mom thrive or show commitment and energy during my childhood?
- What areas seemed more difficult for her when it came to her energy levels?

Prompts for Discussion with Your Mom

- What parts of my childhood do you remember being the most difficult to handle energy-wise?
- What helps you when you're feeling exhausted and overwhelmed? That might be rest and quiet, darkness and solitude, or activities and interests you love.

Accept

It Wasn't Your Fault

It's easy to think that parenting you and/or your sibling(s) was the primary cause of your mother's stress and burnout. Hopefully the information in this chapter is helping you see the complexity of energy use for Autistic people so you can acknowledge that burnout is not specifically caused by parenting. It's caused by years and years of living in an environment that isn't designed for you. Your mother likely did her best to plan and use her energy in the best way she knew how, and you did your best to interpret those choices with the maturity and knowledge you had at the time.

Accepting Two Truths at Once

You might be grappling with a Both/And statement (see Chapter 2) about your childhood that's hard to reconcile: On one hand, your mother was trying to find enough energy to function in a world that wasn't designed for her. On the other hand, you might not have gotten the support you needed from her at times because her energy was so drained. Acknowledging that both things are true can help you reframe the situation and find compassion for both of you. It might help you unpack how you feel about this dichotomy by finding a phrase that resonates with your experience, maybe using it as a writing prompt or even expressing it to your mom. Perhaps something like, "She was doing her best to maintain her energy, *and* I needed more of her attention," or "Mom often cried very easily, which helped her regulate herself, *and* seeing her cry upset me deeply."

The coping mechanisms your mother used to manage low energy levels or Autistic burnout, like being alone or wanting silence, were ways for her to survive. That behavior was likely not a reflection of her interest in you, or even a reflection of her personality traits. When a person is in survival mode, physically or emotionally shutting down is not usually a conscious choice. Finding compassion for her situation can help you see these behaviors in a different light, acknowledge that your mother likely did the best she could, and let go of any guilt you may carry because you thought it was somehow your fault.

Take Energy Levels Into Account When Planning Events

Now that you know more about how your mother has been dealing with her energy levels, you can use that information to plan future events for the two of you. Before the event, you can talk to your mom about what you'd like to plan and how you might be able to work together to arrange something that would be compatible with her energy.

You can ask questions relevant to the event, such as:

- "I'd like to go to the flea market with you. What kind of social energy would an event like that require from you?"
- "Is there a certain time of day to plan an event like this that would work better for your energy levels? Would you rather go early, or maybe after the crowds have died down?"
- "Would it help to take breaks away from people during the event? Or can we agree on a signal for when you're ready to leave?"
- "Would earplugs or dark sunglasses help at an event like this?"

Of course, it's not your job to make sure she's 100 percent happy, and you might not be able to accommodate every request. In that case, you and your mom can make the best decision for yourselves about how to move forward with attending. Maybe it's just not a comfortable scenario for her at all and you pick another event, or perhaps a smaller, quieter version of that event would work best at a future date. But making an effort to be curious and conciliatory can go a long way to showing that you're trying to meet her in the middle because you genuinely enjoy her company.

Remember That You're Only Responsible for Yourself

While you are doing the hard work of learning how to show you care deeply about your mom, remember it isn't your sole responsibility to make her feel comfortable and happy wherever she goes. Environments are felt differently by everyone there, and you can't control someone else's experience. You should also enjoy the event in your own way and not take on the responsibility of making sure that your mom is happy at all times. That is *her* responsibility. Of course, being honest and open with one another is a great step in trying to make sure everyone's needs are met. This approach may establish a new level of trust and understanding.

Knowing that she is seen and that you're attempting to understand her could go a long way. However, you get to have experiences that meet your own needs too, and it's important not to worry about making sure that everything aligns with your mother's preferences all the time. Like we've discussed, she is an adult who has been living in the world long before you came along, and she can likely tell if she needs to take a break or leave a situation. Just the fact that you're taking her feelings into account and checking in with her is a wonderful step in showing your love for her.

Respect Boundaries

Even if you try to plan an event cooperatively, sometimes it's just not possible to make things mutually agreeable. Maybe you play in a rock band and your mother has a hard time with loud noises. Maybe you're a morning person and prefer a 7 a.m. exercise class, but your mom is more energetic at night and wants the 7 p.m. option. Sometimes the gap is just too far to bridge—and that's okay.

Instead of pushing either one of you to do something that makes you uncomfortable, try to accept that you or your mother might not want to attend certain events together. Either of you can set a boundary and communicate that some part of the event is not going to work for you, and that's both a healthy and considerate choice. Autistic women tend to appreciate clarity and open communication, so just tell her what you've decided. Maybe you can say, "Mom, I'd love you to be at that class, but I know that isn't your favorite thing to do and doesn't make you feel your best. How about you and I do something we'd both enjoy next week?" Or "Mom, I'd rather you didn't come to that class with me. You don't like the music, and I think it makes it hard for both of us to enjoy. What about we do a board game tomorrow together? That is something you and I both have fun doing and can be our best selves at."

If the event is particularly important to either of you, and you decide not to do it together, try to plan a separate time that works for both of you to meet and talk about how it went. You can bond while sharing photos, stories, or mementos of the event after the fact, which is an easy way to connect over your experience.

A Mom's Perspective

"I appreciate it when my kids let me sit things out without taking it personally, because it's never about not wanting to be with them. I just can't always handle the places that they want to be. But I still want to hear how it went!"
—Lynn, 68

Appreciate

Trying to See a New Perspective

We can all understand feeling exhausted. But gaining a deeper understanding of your Autistic mother's energy levels through learning about Spoon Theory and Autistic burnout can take some time, compassion, and thoughtful reflection to fully process. Understanding someone else's nervous system is of course a challenging task, especially if your mother does not share a lot of her thoughts with you.

What may be helpful is to think about the ways in which your mother did show up for you, and consider how much it may have taken a lot out of her to do so. As an adult, you can likely see the various roles your mother may have held throughout your childhood. Maybe she had a professional career in addition to being a parent. Maybe she was a caretaker of other family members, or had a role in the community. In any case, parenting is a lot of hard work, and your mother likely had to balance the demands of parenting with her Autistic energy needs.

Understanding your mother's energy levels doesn't erase how you experienced your childhood or continue to experience your adulthood. The hope is that it feels less heavy, and there is some room for considering another perspective.

Finding Common Ground

Whether you're a parent or not, and whether you're neurodivergent or not, we all experience feelings of overwhelm, exhaustion, and stress. But the source and intensity of that stress can vary based on how our brains are wired. When you were a child, your mom's energy levels may have seemed like a reaction to you or your siblings. As an adult, you can likely recognize that living in a demanding world is hard. Even if you don't have kids, you can probably see how parenting makes it harder, and even if you're neurotypical, you can now understand how being Autistic makes everyday life even more impactful on your body. Understanding how sensory load and communication differences affected your mom's energy levels can make it all feel a lot less personal.

At the same time, finding common ground with your mom as a fellow adult in a stressful world can help you approach each other with more patience. Give both yourself and her a bit of a break. It may have hurt as a child, and that is not going to change, but as an adult you now hopefully understand something that only time could teach you; life is tough for us all, and coping with it takes a lot of strength. Normalizing the feeling of being overwhelmed can help you reduce the need to place blame.

The Gift of Prioritizing Rest

You are likely carrying forward some important lessons from your mother's management of her energy levels. Maybe you're very attuned to other people's energy levels. You might be quick to help someone feel comfortable and welcome, or know how to rest without reason or explanation. If your mom was able to rest when she was tired, she might have taught you that productivity isn't always the highest priority in life, which can be a real gift. Maybe you have strong self-reflection skills and know what your body needs.

If you are quick to take care of yourself and avoid burnout, some of that technique might have come from growing up around your mother doing the same thing. If not, see if you can incorporate any of those skills into your life now. So many people today focus on multitasking and pushing themselves past exhaustion. Could you use a break to replenish your spoons? Ask yourself which activities you engage in drain your energy and which give you a boost. You don't need to wait until you're nearly burned out to take care of yourself. Use what you've learned in this chapter as a gift to yourself on improving the way you manage your own energy.

Prompts for Self-Reflection

- How did I interpret my mom's energy levels when I was a child?
- Do I feel any differently now, considering what I know about masking, Spoon Theory, and energy regulation?

Key Takeaways

- Autistic burnout is a serious, chronic form of physical exhaustion.
- Shutdowns and meltdowns can also happen as a result of ongoing masking or from being sensorily overwhelmed.
- It was likely a combination of many things that impacted your mother's energy levels. It wasn't just from parenting you and/or your sibling(s), and how she handled low energy levels was not your fault.
- Setting boundaries and having clear communication about energy can be incredibly helpful for both you and your mom.
- Understanding your mom's struggle with exhaustion and burnout may help you take better care of yourself and others, and appreciate the importance and benefits of rest.

Chapter 8

Organization, Planning, and Preparation:

Respecting the Executive Functioning Demands on Mothers

Executive functioning (EF) refers to the brain's ability to engage in goal-directed behavior. It includes skills like attention and focus, short-term memory, planning, organization, time management, task initiation, follow-through, and the ability to shift between tasks when needed. These skills allow a person to decide what needs to be done next, break tasks into manageable steps, estimate how long they will take, adjust when something doesn't go as planned, and move flexibly from one demand to the next. EF skills rely on how different brain regions connect and coordinate. In Autistic brains, coordination between these brain regions can be organized and timed differently. So the way Autistic peoples' brains are wired makes EF tasks especially challenging—and motherhood adds dozens of EF tasks to a person's plate. This tricky combination means that your mother might have trouble planning and executing tasks, switching focus, or following through, which may impact your relationship.

This chapter will explain what happens at the intersection of executive functioning skills, autism, and motherhood, and help you:

- **Understand** the vast number of EF tasks that are placed on mothers and how Autistic women handle them.
- **Accept** that people who don't excel at EF tasks aren't lazy, unmotivated, or uncaring.
- **Appreciate** that you might have become more independent and goal-oriented as you filled in your mother's EF gaps growing up.

This chapter will offer some sobering perspectives on the amount that has been asked of her as a mother, and will help you make sense of the coping methods she may have used to accomplish everything she could.

Understand

The Brain's Operating System

Most of us rely on EF constantly, often without realizing it. Consider something as routine as scheduling a doctor's appointment. You must remember the task, find time to make the call, check your calendar, coordinate availability, schedule the appointment, plan transportation, and estimate how long the entire process will take. The same is true for daily tasks like making dinner—knowing when to start cooking, what ingredients are needed, what steps to follow, and how to time everything so the meal is ready before bedtime. Each step of those tasks requires a whole range of EF skills:

- Prioritizing what tasks need to get done first.
- Planning something from start to finish.
- Sequencing what order the steps should follow.
- An awareness of how long each task will take.
- Cognitive flexibility to pivot when necessary.
- Use of working memory to hold information for short periods of time.
- Problem-solving to address issues and obstacles.

These tasks can be tough for anyone, but most people can achieve them when they really focus. For many Autistic individuals, however, EF is particularly challenging. This situation seems to happen for one of two reasons:

1. Research suggests that EF tasks can require a lot more cognitive effort for Autistic people. EF depends heavily on the part of the brain that helps manage thoughts, behavior, and decisions—and its coordination with other brain regions. Differences in how these networks function and are organized can make these tasks more demanding for Autistic people. They are intelligent,

motivated, and caring—their brains are just wired differently, and completing EF tasks does not always come easily.

2. Some Autistic people have intact EF skills; others need more support. Yet others may have these skills but they have trouble *accessing* them when they are in sensory overload or Autistic burnout. Either way, the topic of EF is a common issue for Autistic mothers.

Coping Strategies

In order to do her best with EF tasks, your mother likely developed strategies to mitigate any overwhelm she felt. She may have:

- Leaned heavily on routines.
- Made lists to keep track of everything.
- Avoided certain experiences or tasks that were especially challenging.
- Needed extra time to transition between activities.
- Become stressed when plans changed unexpectedly.

When you were a child, these strategies may have felt rigid, limiting, or frustrating—and it's understandable if you sometimes felt controlled, disappointed, or like there wasn't much room for flexibility. At the same time, these strategies were likely her way of managing everything she had on her mind and trying to function as best she could.

A Mom's Perspective

"At sixteen, I saw learning to drive and getting a license as both an exciting privilege and a non-negotiable responsibility. At the time, and for much of my adult life, I did not understand that maintaining a vehicle and navigating daily transportation carried an atypical energy cost for me. Vehicle ownership requires executive function for tracking licenses, registrations, excise taxes, insurance payments, inspections, repairs. Driving itself is an unpredictable multisensory experience. Sirens, horns, engine noise,

GPS directions. Bright sunlight, headlight glare, flashing lights, construction zones. Physical awareness adds another layer. I must calibrate pressure on pedals, keep the car centered in a lane, judge distance while parking, adjust to sudden speed changes, turn to check blind spots, and navigate stop-and-go traffic. It's so much executive functioning all at once. Recently, through parenting a neurodivergent child, I have begun to understand my own neurodivergence more clearly. I now have language to explain why transportation tasks require far more energy and mindfulness for me than they might for a neurotypical parent. Understanding this allows me to recognize the immense invisible work I have done to keep my life moving."

—Sarah, 55

Motherhood-Related Executive Functioning Demands

EF demands increase dramatically with parenthood. Parenting requires constant forward-thinking and coordination—preparing meals and snacks, managing appointments, handling paperwork, organizing school schedules, remembering special events, coordinating transportation, and anticipating children's needs, just to name a few. These demands are ongoing, layered, often invisible—and largely completed by mothers.

For an Autistic mother with EF differences, this load can be overwhelming. Many of the tasks of parenting also require juggling multiple steps, shifting attention quickly, and responding to interruptions. These are precisely the areas that are already especially challenging for an Autistic person. When EF demands are unrelenting, everyday nuisances like small schedule disruptions can feel completely destabilizing.

You might notice signs that EF skills do not come easily to your mother, even if you didn't always have the vocabulary or knowledge to recognize that it was "executive functioning." Perhaps she was often late picking you up—not because she didn't prioritize you, but because time estimation and task completion were difficult. Or perhaps she couldn't start her day without making a list of everything that needed doing, and you had to wait while she figured it all out. These patterns may have felt inflexible or confusing, but they served as her coping strategies—ways to reduce the cognitive and sensory overload of EF tasks.

The following is a breakdown of some common EF tasks, how they can look for an Autistic person, and how they look for a child in that environment.

EF Skill	Why It Is an Important Skill	Functional Impact If That Skill Is Not a Strength	How This May Have Looked When You Were a Child
Task Initiation	Allows a person to begin tasks, even when they feel overwhelming or uninteresting.	Tasks may be delayed or avoided, especially when they feel complex or draining.	It seemed like things didn't get started unless there was pressure or urgency.
Planning	Helps organize steps and anticipate what needs to happen next.	Daily activities may feel either strict and scheduled or chaotic and last-minute.	Plans felt inflexible, or unclear, rushed, and stressful.
Organization	Supports managing items like belongings, paperwork, and schedules.	Items get misplaced; paperwork or details may be missed.	Permission slips, school items, or materials were forgotten.

Time Management	Helps estimate timing, helps you arrive when expected.	Chronic lateness and/or trouble with transitions; or perpetual punctuality.	Pickups happened late, mornings felt frantic, or schedules felt unpredictable; or schedules were rigid and uncompromising.
Working Memory	Holds information in mind while completing tasks.	Instructions or details may be forgotten mid-task.	You had to remind her repeatedly or you felt responsible for remembering things.
Task Switching (Cognitive Flexibility)	Allows moving between tasks or adapting to change.	Difficulty shifting attention or adjusting plans.	She seemed "stuck," upset by changes, or slow to respond.
Prioritization	Helps decide what matters most when demands compete.	Urgent needs may not be addressed first.	It felt like the "wrong things" got her attention.
Problem-Solving	Supports adjusting when things go off plan.	Small disruptions may feel overwhelming.	Minor issues became big moments of stress.

There are a few subsets of EF tasks that come up again and again for mothers, such as school and social needs. Let's take a deeper look at those.

School and Health

Helping manage a child's school experience and medical needs often falls on mothers. Think of all the related details that require EF skills:

- Signing forms and permission slips, filling out medical histories, dealing with insurance companies
- Scheduling and attending medical appointments
- Giving children reminders for things like returning library books, sneakers for gym class, and picture day
- Reading and responding to communications from teachers or doctors
- Being aware of and attending in-person events like concerts, conferences, and special celebrations
- Dealing with shifting school schedules like late starts, half days, and school vacations

If any of these examples resonate with you, you may recall difficult moments like being called out in front of the class for having unsubmitted forms, the sting of forgotten items or missed events, or the stress of last-minute scrambles to get to the dentist on time. This may have felt embarrassing, stressful, or even neglectful at the time—and those feelings are still valid. Understanding these moments through an EF lens can offer context for why they happened, while still honoring how they affected you. These events often reflect an overload on your mother's EF demands, not a lack of love or care.

Cooking

Food preparation is another area that requires strong EF focus. Cooking requires planning, sequencing, and time management—and when sensory demands like smells, textures, and noise are added, it can quickly become overwhelming.

If meals felt stressful or repetitive in your home as a child, this could be why. You may remember very rigid meal routines: the same dinners on the same days, meals served at the same time regardless of circumstances, or strict expectations about seating. These coping strategies may have helped your mother take care of you while reducing her already strained cognitive load.

A Child's Perspective

"My mother always seemed overwhelmed by simple tasks that looked easy for everyone else. Switching plans was often the thing that could really throw off our day. I used to interpret this as her rigidity and control as incredibly hard and annoying. Now I understand how deeply executive functioning impacts everyday life."
—Ava, 26

Social Life

As we've discussed, moms also hold a lot of the responsibility to schedule and coordinate social experiences for their children, which requires EF skills *and* social skills. There's schedule planning, organizing to leave on time and meet up, and the social niceties that are part of reaching out to other moms to coordinate playdates. These skills might not have come naturally to your mom, or she may have felt judged by mom groups for how she showed up and interacted with them. If your mom was overwhelmed by EF tasks, you might not have felt comfortable asking to invite friends over to play very often.

Our Story

Growing up, it felt like we were always *almost* on time. My mother was constantly starting one task, setting it down, and picking up another. Papers covered the table: mail, permission slips, notes she meant to read. She always knew what needed to be done, but the order of it seemed hard for her to hold on to. There was often a lot of clutter.

Mornings were the hardest. I'd be ready at the door, watching the clock, while she finished "one more thing." Sometimes we made it on time; sometimes we didn't. When we were late, I assumed it meant I wasn't the priority.

Dinner followed a consistent pattern. Meals were repetitive

> and scheduled. Monday's meal was always the same. So was Tuesday's. If plans changed, she became tense or quiet. I learned not to ask for flexibility. It felt safer to fit myself into her routines than to risk the stress that came with change. As a child, I saw this as her personality. She was disorganized, rigid, and overwhelmed. I didn't have another explanation.
>
> Years later, I understand that my mother was managing more than I could see. Planning, starting, stopping, shifting attention. All that executive function took energy. By the end of the day especially, there was nothing left. She wasn't careless with time or uninterested. She was working against a system that demanded constant organization and multitasking. We were almost on time, not because she didn't care, but because getting there took more than anyone realized.
>
> —Jack, 36

Navigating signing children up for activities is another social area of parenting that carries EF demands. From sorting out details of sports seasons to finding summer camps months ahead of time, a lot of work goes into getting children into extracurricular options. If you felt like you missed out on activities, your world might have seemed limited or isolating. That can be a very upsetting situation for a child. As you reflect on this now, you might begin to see how these tasks placed significant demands on your mother's nervous system and cognitive resources—while still honoring how limiting or isolating that experience felt for you.

Hyperfocus

Another cognitive theory of autism that's related to EF is the concept called monotropism. This is the idea that Autistic minds focus very deeply on one thing at a time, rather than spreading the attention across many things—in other words, a hyperfocus. It's like a spotlight that is shining brightly on one area of interest while the rest of the room is out of focus or dim. Neuroscientists and psychologists believe this happens because the brain finds subjects or stimuli that are of great interest to a person to be deeply rewarding. Monotropism can also act as a kind of filtering mechanism that helps Autistic brains reduce the overload from the rest of the world. Highly focused interests are also predictable and structured, which can feel comforting to a brain that might have a different way of processing fast-changing environments.

This type of focus can be a real strength, as this level of concentration brings deep thinking, creativity, and a close attention to details. It can also elicit great joy, breed expertise, and even power breakthroughs. In today's world of short videos and instant gratification, monotropism is becoming a coveted ability. However, it can also make it hard to switch attention to another task—and multitasking is a significant part of parenting. Maybe you noticed that your mother couldn't take her attention away from a good book, an interesting documentary, or an activity she enjoys like drawing or painting. This does not signify a disinterest in you or your life; it's a neurological difference in shifting focus.

Executive Functioning, Sensory Processing, and Energy Levels Together

Executive functioning does not operate in isolation. It is deeply affected by both sensory processing systems and energy levels. When sensory input—noise, touch, smells, visual clutter—is overwhelming, executive functioning skills becomes even harder to execute. Likewise, EF tasks require energy, or spoons (see Chapter 7 for more on Spoon Theory). Sometimes taking part in special interests can restore someone's energy levels; sometimes it can take all their energy due to the intense focus it takes. If EF tasks were high energy-drainers for your mother, she might have limited how many other EF tasks she took on. This may have meant being highly fixated on learning about animals, but that meant having fewer spoons available for making dinner, organizing the next day's to-do list, or discussing your day at school. While there may have been reasons for these limitations, it's okay if it still felt like something important was missing for you.

Prompts for Self-Reflection

- Were tasks often missed or delayed during my childhood, or was my mom organized and into routines?
- How did her being late and disorganized/on time and inflexible impact me as a child?
- How does my mindset change when I think of those moments through an Autistic EF lens?

Prompts for Discussion with Your Mom

- Are any EF tasks particularly challenging for you? Which ones?
- What do you wish I knew about how you handle EF tasks?

Accept

Reframing Your Perspective

In a society that values neurotypical brain wiring, people with EF differences can feel judged and criticized. Living in a neurotypical world can feel exhausting and overwhelming for many reasons—and when an Autistic person is in that overwhelmed state, EF tasks are extremely difficult to take on. These challenges are not a personality flaw. Your mom likely isn't lazy or scattered or unreliable—rather, her body and mind feel overworked trying to exist as a neurodivergent person in a world set up with an expectation of neurotypicality.

Reframing your childhood through an Autistic EF lens does not erase the impact of what you experienced, or might still experience with your mom. But it can offer some people a new perspective. There may have been times when your needs were not met, and this could have caused you real emotional harm. Reflecting on how and why this harm happened may help soften the emotions around these experiences. You might try thinking of statements that capture your initial experiences with your mother's EF skills, and your thoughts about it now that you have a different perspective. Here are some examples.

Statement	Feelings	Reframed Perspective
When I was eight, I didn't get to play baseball because my mother missed the sign-ups.	Being left out, disappointment, anger.	Baseball sign-ups happened in the middle of winter holidays, which is an extremely busy time filled with EF demands. My mom did get me into karate in the summer.

We are still always late for events when I go with my mom.	Embarrassment, frustration.	Planning what time to begin getting ready is an EF task that's particularly difficult for my mom. Now that I understand this, I can help her plan around it or adjust how I approach making plans with her.
Dinner was always the same dish served at the same time.	Annoyance, frustration.	This system helped my mom always prepare meals for us. I was glad we got to eat together each night.
I never had playdates or friends over to my house.	Confusion, anger, resentment.	I realize now the demands and stress social organization put on my mom, and how she did her best to figure out ways I could enjoy playing as a child.
We never did more than one "event" each day or week.	Anger, boredom, confusion.	Her low tolerance for events allowed us to prioritize making the one weekly event fun and special, and I didn't feel overwhelmed or overscheduled when I was young.

Work Together to Address Current Needs

While it may not be your responsibility to fully care for your mom, you might want to offer to help her with some EF tasks. If so, it's best to ask first if she would like your help, as she may prefer to do these things on her own or in her own way. It's also helpful for you if you only offer her the energy and time you can truly give without burning yourself out, so ensure you've gauged what you can realistically do for her without sacrificing your own life.

With these points in mind, this could be a good opportunity for you and your mom to talk about each of your limits and share expectations for what each of you can handle, EF-wise. It's easy to make assumptions about each other, but talking and listening may help you better understand how each other is experiencing the world. Here are some sample conversation starters:

- "Mom, I'm worried that you're not seeing a doctor as regularly as you should be. I want you to be healthy and well looked after. Is there anything stopping you from going? Would it help if I made the appointment for you? You can give me a few general days and times that would work for your schedule this month before I call."
- "Mom, you mentioned that you wanted to sit together at the next family event. Let's arrive at 6 p.m. so we can find seats next to each other. It's an hour away, so we need to leave by 5 p.m. That means we should start getting ready at 4 p.m. Does that make sense? And does that work?"
- "Mom, I notice some mail piling up on the counter. I have some free time next week—can I come over to help you sort through it?"

Talking through these needs will allow for careful planning and getting necessary tasks complete. It will also let her know that you care and are on hand to help her with the EF skills she may find more difficult, like planning, organization, and follow-through, if she needs and wants it. Try to approach these topics in a nonjudgmental way, and keep an open mind about what her preferred solutions might be. Of course, you don't need to try to do everything for your mother, either. Next, we'll talk about setting boundaries when necessary.

Setting Appropriate Boundaries

Accepting your mother's EF skills also involves recognizing what is *not* your responsibility. You are not responsible for fully taking on your mom's executive functioning tasks, organizing her life, or compensating for her limits. You can be compassionate about what she's going through, and also not take on all her duties.

It's nice if you want to help her, and if she's accepting of your help. But at the same time, you are allowed to set boundaries around what you can and cannot tolerate, even as you show understanding and love. Healthy adult relationships often require stepping out of old roles. As a child, you may have always been the one to remind, organize, or plan. Now you can think about allowing each person to take responsibility for themselves where possible, and helping out where you're able. See if any of these examples spark an idea for your life.

Previous Responsibility	New Boundary
I always schedule our family birthday dinners—find a mutually agreeable time, make a reservation, invite people, and so on.	Going forward, I can communicate clearly what responsibilities I am able to take on for birthday dinners, and request that others take on the remaining tasks involved.
I apologize to others on my mother's behalf if she is late.	I will stop apologizing for her. I will remind myself that I'm not responsible for her actions, or what other people think of her lateness.
I always clean up all the clutter and organize Mom's space when I'm at her home.	I will start checking in to see if she'd like support before just cleaning up. She may not be overwhelmed with the space in the ways that I am.

I always remind my mother about her upcoming appointments or things she needs to remember to do.	If she wants my support, I can teach Mom how to set reminders on her phone, and I will trust that she can deal with the consequences of any missed appointments. I will ask if she needs any more help than that.

The process of setting boundaries with yourself and an Autistic family member is deeply personal. It may take time to implement changes, but these adjustments are meant to help you release the feeling of responsibility and the stresses of endless caretaking so you can find a better way for both of you to exist. It can feel uncomfortable at first, especially if these roles were established early. But it can also create space for a more balanced relationship.

Appreciate

Different Brain Wiring Leads to New Ideas

So much of the general conversation about EF skills is framed in a negative light—"struggles," "deficits," or "inabilities." And EF differences *can* feel challenging at times. But thinking differently also leads to out-of-the-box brainstorming, creative solutions, and incredible innovation. Neurodivergent people are well represented among innovators, likely because their brains make unusual connections and they are comfortable challenging the status quo.

Even if you don't think of your mother as an "innovator," your relationship with her might help you recognize that different brain wiring is not automatically "bad." With that mentality, you are more likely to listen to all voices, give novel ideas a chance, and have a more open mind. For example, Greta Thunberg is an Autistic environmental advocate. Her brain has developed innovative ways to fight climate change. Similarly, Temple Grandin, author of *Thinking in Pictures*, is an animal welfare advocate and scientist who has developed more humane cattle practices that have supported the farming industry. These unique brains have changed the way we think about important subjects.

Skills You Learned

If your mother had EF differences, you might have gained a few highly valuable skills, both from watching her and from your effort to help her out. While in this kind of environment, you might have:

- Learned a strong sense of independence.
- Become flexible and adaptable.
- Developed strong problem-solving skills.
- Created your own systems for remembering things.
- Seen the value in the systems and routines that your mother created.

You might be able to appreciate these helpful traits now that you have this lens. While they don't erase any difficult moments of your childhood, they are part of what makes you unique, and part of the love your mother gave you.

Prompts for Self-Reflection

- What new insights on executive functioning do I have?
- How can I use these insights to improve my relationship with my mother?

Key Takeaways

- EF differences affect planning, time management, and follow-through, often making parenting tasks even more demanding.
- What might have looked like inconsistency and disorganization in your Autistic mom could have been the result of overload, limited energy, and difficulty accessing EF skills, not from lack of care.
- Understanding EF more fully allows you to separate your mother's limitations from her intentions.
- Acceptance doesn't excuse the harm, but it may help you recognize that her coping strategies—perhaps routines, avoidance, and rigidity—were ways to get the jobs done.
- Growing up alongside someone with neurodivergent EF approaches likely gave you your own skills, like adaptability, independence, and understanding limitations.

Chapter 9

Family Harmony:

Improving Family Dynamics

To better understand your mother, it helps to think about the family you grew up in. Families come in all shapes and sizes, and regardless of exactly what yours looks like, your mother has likely had a significant impact on how you experienced family life. Of course, your family dynamic included your relationship with your mom, but maybe it also included a relationship with other parents, siblings, extended family—and your mother had relationships with those people too. This chapter will examine everyone's role in the family, and how autism intersected with these relationships. You may also be Autistic or neurodivergent, or have siblings who are as well, which can further impact family dynamics.

This chapter will help you reflect on these roles and relationships, and:

- **Understand** how autism can influence undercurrents of family dynamics.
- **Accept** that family life can be complicated and still loving.
- **Appreciate** how your family shows love, even if it's different from what you see elsewhere.

As you read this chapter, you may experience many strong feelings when thinking about your family. Know that there is no "right" way to feel, and that your emotions are valid, even if they are conflicting at times. Instead of focusing on blame, try to open your mind to these new outlooks that can help you all grow together as a family.

Understand

Family Structure

Every family is unique, and family structures and caregiving roles can vary widely. Regardless of the structure, it's usually true that members of a family adopt roles, often without realizing it. Common roles include the peacemaker, the responsible one, the rebel, the translator, the independent one, and the quiet observer.

These roles, while they may have been established quite early in your family, do not necessarily mean that they are permanent. These family roles are influenced by several factors, such as:

- Birth order
- Personalities
- Temperament
- How adults engaged with each other
- How your siblings engaged with each other
- Personal histories and life experiences
- Cultural practices and common roles

As mentioned, the roles we play in our families don't have to be static—they often fluctuate over time depending on everyone's ages and circumstances.

A Mom's Perspective

"As a middle-aged Autistic woman, my experience parenting eleven-year-old twin boys is defined by a sensory and emotional intensity that often feels insurmountable. While I am a college professor capable of managing a mortgage and a career, the interpersonal demands of parenting non-Autistic but highly oppositional children leave me in a state of constant depletion. My boys have ADHD and are frequently defiant and verbally abusive; my daily life is less about nurturing and more about surviving the

tumult until bedtime. When my children are home, my professional focus vanishes, replaced by the need to minimize conflict and survive the afternoon. In this environment, typical parental expectations—like supervising homework—feel impossible. My priority is often just managing the fallout from their meltdowns."
—Helen, 63

Sibling Dynamics with an Autistic Mother

If you have siblings, the way that your siblings experienced your Autistic mother may not have been exactly the same as you. This situation is common in all families, but may have an extra layer when thinking about your mother as an Autistic woman. You and your siblings might compare memories and find that all of you have different experiences, opinions, and even judgments about these moments. For example, you may look back on your childhood and see the complexities of adult life that your parents went through, and notice how your younger years may have been impacted by your mom's difference in brain wiring. You may think your mom was likely doing her very best.

At the same time, your sibling may remember how painful that time was, and may still hold your mother responsible for falling short sometimes. They may even find themselves still struggling to understand her choices and actions. Both can be true simultaneously: Your mom was doing her best *and* the way she parented at times didn't always meet her children's needs. Also, you don't have to agree with your siblings' interpretations in order for your own experience to be real and meaningful. Different perspectives can coexist, and your experience is still yours to understand in your own way.

Handling Conflict

Many Autistic women say they tend to avoid conflict, which can be overwhelming. You may have noticed that your mother handled sibling conflict differently than other parents you know. She may have shied away from it, taken on one of her children's emotions, been rigid and strict with her rules, or become quickly overwhelmed. This may have been most evident when you or your siblings (either as children or adults) had emotional outbursts or fought, and your mother needed to provide emotional regulation, discipline, or conflict resolution. Plus, siblings often have a unique superpower of knowing exactly how to "push your buttons," which can escalate these tensions.

Managing these conflicts can be exhausting and challenging for any parent, but the impact of noise, the quick back-and-forth of verbal exchanges, and the shifting perspectives may have been especially hard for your mother to navigate. Autistic people need to use a lot of physical and cognitive energy to receive all that input, and they may not get the time they need to respond due to the frantic energy and feelings of overwhelm. Your mother may have avoided these conflicts altogether, leaving you or your siblings feeling abandoned. Or, she may have felt pressured to choose one side or another, which could have worsened the conflict. If that happened, you and your siblings may have had to parent yourselves in these moments. Even if there were reasons it was difficult for your mother, it's okay to recognize how much that asked of you as a child.

A Mom's Perspective

"The psychological toll of parenting is compounded by my own Autistic traits, specifically my inability to handle opposition. In intense interpersonal relationships, I often just give in because I cannot withstand the conflict. This makes placing limits on my children's behavior an agonizing struggle. My children have even mocked me for sobbing, which I do often out of sheer overwhelm. I feel a deep sense of failure when I compare myself to neurotypical standards of supervision and discipline."
—Rita, 68

Sibling-to-Sibling Relationships

Parents always have slightly different relationships with each of their children. These differences can sometimes lead to resentments among siblings. For example, maybe your mother seemed to connect more strongly with one of your siblings than with you, or vice versa. Whether or not this situation was true, or it just *felt* true to one of you, it likely felt upsetting, confusing, and problematic for you as a child and potentially even now as an adult. This history may impact how you feel toward your sibling even today. On the other hand, having an Autistic mother might also have bonded you strongly with your sibling(s). You may see your mom through similar lived experiences, and find it comforting to have someone else who understands the complexities of your childhood.

Reconciling What You Learned from Your Mom with What's Best for You Now

All children learn a lot from their parents: the good, the bad, and everything in between. So much of who we are as adults is directly related to our childhood experiences and our parents. Many aspects of adult life will be strongly influenced by the environment in which you were raised, like:

- How you engage with your friends, your partner, or even your own children.
- Your preferred conflict or argument style.
- The approaches you take to managing stress.
- How you express your emotions.

Once you are grown, however, it's valuable to reflect on whether the styles you learned from your parents are actually the best ones for you to carry forward. Here are some examples of how the behaviors and actions you saw as a child might not align with what you know about yourself now:

Your Mother's Style	Your Style
Your mother may prefer to quietly disagree with someone instead of arguing.	You may prefer a heated debate with lots of eye contact to hash out an issue.
Your mother may have had a strict adherence to rules for her kids.	You would rather be flexible and have discussions about rules for your kids.
Your mother may like listening to loud music and fidgeting to reduce her stress.	You may like reading quietly alone to reduce your stress.

As you can see, one living style is not better than the other—they are simply different. But it's very easy to automatically adopt your parents' approaches because those are the conditions you became familiar with in childhood. As you learn more about your Autistic mother, it's a good time to ask yourself whether the tendencies you learned from her also truly work for you or not. This isn't an all-or-nothing exercise—you can pick and choose which behaviors resonate with you and which you'd like to do differently. You can respect your mother's choices while also being an independent adult and making your own.

Understanding an Autistic Sibling

Since autism runs in families, you may have grown up with a sibling who is also Autistic. Since all Autistic people are different, it's hard to speak to exactly what that experience may have been like for you, but I'll try to address the topic in general terms.

"Needs"/"Functioning" Vocabulary

As discussed in Chapter 1, describing Autistic people as "low functioning" and "high functioning" is limiting and potentially insulting. It doesn't account for the dynamic nature of this neurotype and the intersectional lived experiences. However, the terms "low support needs" and "high support needs" are currently the most acceptable descriptors used by the Autistic community.

Life As a Neurotypical Sibling

Neurodivergence tends to run in families, so it's possible your mom wasn't the only Autistic person in your childhood home. If you're neurotypical and had an Autistic sibling, regardless of their exact profile of autism, there was likely more time and attention devoted to your sibling as your parent(s) tried to navigate their needs. Having a sibling with "high support needs"—meaning that they may have significant cognitive differences, significant differences with communication (language understanding and use), motor challenges (e.g., walking, eating), and significant sensory processing needs—looks very different from having a sibling with "low support needs," where they may have "normative" cognitive and language skills, but have challenges with social engagement or executive functioning. Research tells us that neurotypical siblings of Autistic siblings have some commonalties in their experiences. On one hand, the neurotypical siblings tend to have strong flexibility, understanding of differences, and patience and compassion for disabilities. On the other hand, many neurotypical siblings report a lower amount of time and attention given to them by parents, a difference in discipline, and the constant need to be flexible with family decisions being made primarily around their Autistic sibling's needs rather than their own. Neurotypical siblings also share that they usually attempted to be the "easy one" who can go with the flow. On top of all that, many carry a lot of concern about the future of their Autistic sibling, from concerns about how they'll fit in at school to worrying about whether they'll have to "take care" of them on top of their own adult needs. These worries can also lead to the neurotypical sibling feeling guilty that they might be "bothered" by caretaking for someone they love. There are so many complex feelings at play, and they are all valid.

Additionally, you may have been taken to countless appointments for your Autistic sibling (e.g., speech therapy, occupational therapy, behavioral therapy) and had to sit in waiting rooms while they received important care. If the family schedule revolved around them, it may have impacted access to your own extracurricular activities or playdates too. Inviting friends over to your house might have also posed a challenge. These experiences can certainly complicate your own feelings toward both your parents and your Autistic sibling, and it's valid if those moments felt overwhelming or isolating.

Some neurotypical children say this dynamic caused them to build resentment toward their mother, feeling as if their Autistic sibling was given more attention or was treated with more care. But that doesn't mean she loved one child more—just that different children require different kinds of support at different times. Most moms aren't playing favorites;

they're simply responding to each child's needs, even if it doesn't always look equal.

Childhood with an Autistic sibling *and* an Autistic mother may have been tough at times, and it will have looked different compared to a neurotypical family. But there were likely upsides to it as well. This kind of childhood experience often helps neurotypical children foster real empathy, maturity, and a deeper appreciation for individual human differences. Many neurotypical siblings say they watched how their mom really understood their Autistic sibling's needs, and they learned how to care for others by seeing this deep connection firsthand. The dynamic between an Autistic sibling and an Autistic mom can also be full of joy; they are often quite in tune. Some family members even report that the two neurodivergent people in their family have their own "language." Even if their Autistic presentations looked different on the surface, research tells us that Autistic communication is quite different that neurotypical communication. If we think back to the Double-Empathy Theory described in Chapter 2, it makes sense that they would communicate more effectively with one another. They may also have overlapping special interests, or have similar reactions to certain sounds. Having someone else in the home who understands them in those ways may have brought harmony to both them and the family unit.

Our Story

My younger brother is Autistic, and when he was diagnosed in his twenties, it helped my mom (in her sixties) understand that she might be Autistic too. Their whole vibe together has always been different from how she connects with me and my sisters. They finish each other's sentences, they obsess over similar topics, they make inside jokes, that kind of thing. As a kid, I thought our brother was just the favorite. After they were both diagnosed, I started to see how sweet and caring their relationship really was.

They both have friends who accepted their "quirks," but it was different having someone in the house who truly got their preferences. For example, my brother can't have his food touching other food—and this wasn't even a concern for my mom. She just got it instantly. No one in the family made my brother feel "weird" for wanting things a certain way like that. It was a very accepting environment. Yes, he needed therapy every week, he needed earplugs at dinner, and he still has to leave the room when our nieces and nephews get too loud. But to this day, no one in the family gives him a hard time about having those needs. Not all Autistic people are that lucky. And that tone was really set by our mom, who innately understood that some kids are simply different from others.

—Jamilla, 40

Single Parenting and Divorce

Some families are from single-parent households, while others have two or more parents, sometimes spread across multiple homes. If you were raised by a single mom, there may be an added layer of complexity to the family dynamic. Both divorce and solo parenting come with a whole host of hurdles your mom may have faced, like having increased emotional stress, less immediate support, less financial security, and more daily responsibility. Divorce is emotionally complex, and Autistic individuals may process emotions differently or need more time and space to do so. Co-parenting also requires a lot of nuanced communication, negotiation, and reading between the lines. If your mom found these kinds of interactions challenging, then communication with a co-parent, lawyers, or school systems may have felt overwhelming or draining. With fewer adults in the household, there tends to be less of a buffer for rest and recovery, so single Autistic moms often have to make difficult choices about where to spend their limited energy—perhaps prioritizing essential tasks over emotional availability, flexibility, or shared activities.

Single parenting is also often supported informally by friends, other parents, and local community members. If your mom had difficulty forming or maintaining those connections, she may have had less support to rely on, which could have meant fewer resources, less help, or more stress on both of you. As a child, you may have noticed these pressures in your day-to-day life. Even if these challenges help explain what your mom was managing, it's natural to recognize how they may have affected you as well. Growing up in a single-parent or divorced household can bring up a wide range of feelings, and it's okay if yours include both empathy for your mom and recognition of what may have been hard for you.

A Child's Perspective

"I thought my mom was failing in her marriage because she was not showing up in the ways that I saw on TV. Really, it was a mismatch: Her communication style didn't match my father's . . . and she also didn't understand her own brain. It's hard to make relationships work when you're trying to just survive each day. I can see that now."

—Kelly, 35

Considering Your Relationship with Your Other Parent

If you grew up in a two-parent household, your relationship with your Autistic mother will likely have felt different from your relationship with your other parent. If you and your other parent are both neurotypical, this bond can often be quite strong. Your other parent often becomes the "bridge" between you and your mom. They can negotiate, understand, and attempt to repair any breakdowns with your mom. They can also often relate to some of your challenges with your mom and can help navigate those situations.

Our Story

I'm the middle child of five kids from England. Our dad was a doctor, and our mum spent most of her life as a baker before becoming a receptionist when we were teenagers. Both careers suited her well—baking required precision and organization, skills she excelled at, while her punctuality, list-making, mental math, and incredible memory made her perfect for secretarial work. She thrived in both roles and genuinely enjoyed working, whether at her job or at home.

Growing up, there were challenges and benefits to having an

Autistic mum, especially before we understood what that meant. Like all kids, I learned from her example, often without realizing it. She was an obsessive worker who insisted on doing all the household chores herself because she believed they had to be done a certain way. As a result, I never developed the habit of cleaning until I moved out and had no choice. She managed everything—meals, clothes, appointments, family gatherings, and extracurriculars—so it often felt like she *could* handle anything. Now, with a family of my own, I've fallen into the same pattern of taking on all the chores, which is exhausting for me and blocks my family from developing independence. I also inherited her anxiety around change, having been subliminally taught that if things don't go to plan, we panic.

Family time could also be tough for her. Around her five loud, argumentative kids, she struggled to verbalize her feelings, often crying at the smallest tension. My younger sibling, who is also Autistic, regularly received more of her attention because she instinctively understood his struggles with overstimulation. This dynamic pushed a wedge between me and her, but it brought me closer to my father, a bond that remains strong today.

Still, my mother set some incredible examples. She showed me it's okay to leave a room if you need some space. She taught me that it's acceptable to cry if you feel overwhelmed. She taught me to be naturally organized and detail-oriented, and I can whip up a meal for seven with no trouble at all. I've also worked hard to learn to confidently express my emotions—something that she showed me is vital for my own happiness. While all childhood has difficulties, adulthood offers us the chance to grow and shape who we want to be based on what we love about what she taught us.

—Lily, 37

In some families, the other parent may also be neurodivergent. We do have some data that shows neurodivergent people often connect with other neurodivergent people, so you could have two neurodivergent parents. Their styles and preferences might be a wonderful complement to each other (they may each have their own "flavor" of neurodivergence, and they work well together). If that's the case, you might still feel a stronger connection with one parent over the other. Or, in other cases, you may feel challenged by both parents, and not understood by either of them most of the time. Every family dynamic is different, of course—what's important is thinking about what parts of your relationship(s) with your parent(s) are working well, and which could use improvement.

Prompts for Self-Reflection

- What roles did I take on in my family? Have these roles evolved or remained the same?
- How did sibling dynamics play out in my family?

Prompts for Discussion with Your Mom

- What part of our family dynamics were most challenging when I was young?
- What do you wish I knew about how you handled sibling dynamics?

Make Your Own Choices

Now that you are an adult, you might not appreciate some of the behaviors or traits you learned from your mother or some of the familial roles you took on as a child. You may struggle to manage stress in healthy ways, or struggle with conflict in relationships. The good news is that you have the power to change these behaviors if they aren't working for you.

As is true for all adults, what's most important is to be self-reflective and try to truly understand yourself. Getting to the root of the issue is always critical, and it allows for a more successful change. For example, let's say you had to be quite independent as a child if your mother wasn't meeting your needs. This trait has likely led to many positive outcomes in your life, such as strong self-esteem and problem-solving skills. On the other hand, you may struggle to ask for help when you need it and take on more responsibilities than you can handle—which leads to overwhelm and stress.

When you can identify these types of nuances, it allows you to:

- More fully understand why you behave the way you do.
- Separate your adult self from your childhood influences.
- Be kinder to yourself by gaining some perspective.
- Look for areas of growth that target exactly what you want to change.

It's tough for many people to look back on their childhoods with an objective eye. Even those with "positive" childhood experiences can discover unexpected thoughts and feelings. Be patient with yourself as you reflect on any changes you'd like to make.

Allow For Contradictory Feelings

Relationships with family members can be complicated under any circumstance. Adding autism to the mix can create additional layers to manage. For example, you may be closer to one parent than the other, or one sibling over others, or if you have an Autistic sibling, they may have a seemingly deeper relationship with your mother than you do. This is all very typical for families.

In addition, it's helpful to recognize that your feelings about your family members might seem contradictory at times. You may feel love, resentment, jealousy, and frustration . . . toward the same single person. You might feel loved and yet still invisible at times. All those feelings can be true, and you might feel them simultaneously. All your feelings are valid, and ones that elicit a lot of emotions may benefit from continued exploration and discussion with your family. Perhaps an individual or family therapist could help you have those conversations. Try to make space for whatever you're feeling, and know that it's okay for seemingly conflicting emotions to coexist.

Use Mutually Agreeable Communication Methods

Before having an emotional conversation with a family member, try to determine each party's preferred communication methods. It's also important to keep in mind that your expectations for conversation (if you are neurotypical) may not align with your mother's. Use the tips in Chapter 5 for effective communication and the ideas in Chapter 4 for emotional expression to create an environment that works for you both.

Enough Love for All

When you think back to your family's dynamics in childhood, you may have felt like you didn't get "enough" of your mother, or your needs weren't met. This is another area where two things can be true at the same time: You might not have had all your needs met, *and* your family was probably doing the best they could, especially if there was limited support, resources, and education or knowledge of autism. Your grief around not being understood and not having your needs met is still real. But staying stuck in this feeling doesn't improve your life or your relationship with your mother or other family members. What *can* improve things is reflecting on your experiences, and then sharing your feelings thoughtfully with your family.

More food for thought: Though it may not always feel like it, most parents love all their children equally. While their expression of love may look different from child to child, parents do love each child the same amount. Try to focus on how your parents did show you love (and vice versa), and speak up if you'd like to see more or less of a certain behavior going forward.

Surrender Your Role As a "Parent"

Children who have complicated childhoods often present as "wise beyond their years" and end up serving as somewhat of a parent themselves at a young age. You may have had more adultlike responsibilities as a child, such as:

- Being emotionally responsible for your mother.
- Taking care of your own needs without the level of support you wanted or needed at that age.
- Preparing your siblings for school or activities.
- Completing a lot of household tasks.

While this situation can build resilience and independence, it can also create some challenges in adulthood. Maybe you struggle to set boundaries or are always trying to people-please. At this point in your life, you can identify why you likely took on this early-parenting role, and you can now tell yourself it's okay to let go of those responsibilities. What you had to be then is not what you have to be now. You can focus on taking care of yourself, which will make you a healthier version of yourself for everyone in your life.

Build an Adult Relationship with Your Siblings

While sibling relationships are sometimes complicated, your siblings are usually the only ones who really "get" what you experienced as a child.

With that can come a special camaraderie and sense of empathy. There is often a deep level of love and understanding among siblings who had the same unique childhood that you did. You may share many of the same traits—or you might all be quite different from each other. You may have experienced your childhoods very differently too, which can be hard when looking back and trying to understand it all. But siblings are the people who can most closely understand your experience of your childhood, and if you're still connected with them, they may be a wonderful lifeline to help you process those times.

You also might approach your relationship with your mother in unique ways. Maybe you can ignore your mother's rigidity around certain things, but your sibling can't—or the other way around. These different approaches can lead to frustration, disagreements, and even conflict. However, you might be able to start a conversation with your sibling about the differences you've noticed, and work together to find common ground or solutions where possible. You and your siblings might be able to delegate tasks that help your mother in areas where she could use support. For example, if your sibling is a great planner, maybe they manage arranging family get-togethers and you take her to doctor's appointments. Try to remember that when it comes to caring for your family, it can help for you and your siblings to work together on the same team.

Sometimes setting boundaries to protect your own mental health is critical. If a sibling's approach to your mom doesn't match at all with yours, it might be best to socialize separately with her. In any case, trying to understand each other, and each other's limits, can make the relationship more harmonious.

Appreciate

Looking Forward

Family dynamics are unique, especially if you grow up with an Autistic mom. With continued understanding of your mother's autism, you may be able to see both your childhood and your adult relationship with your mom in a different light. Whether the path forward involves forgiveness, boundaries, deeper understanding, conversations, or a combination of all those things, you can look for opportunities to strengthen your bond with your mother and the rest of your family.

As you consider any challenges that still exist for you, it's important to also think about how your experience has shaped you in positive ways as well. As a child of an Autistic mother, you've likely learned a great deal that has helped you navigate adulthood. For example, maybe you:

- Approach people and the world with compassion and understanding.
- See strengths in individuals that others miss.
- Think outside the box to problem-solve.
- Have patience for differences.
- Can "read a room" quite well and are attuned to changes in others' emotions and body language.
- Are efficient and thrive independently.
- Are resilient and can adapt to various situations.

These traits are part of who you are, but they were also partially shaped by your mother's influence. Recognizing and respecting *all* the parts of you and your mother is both the joy and challenge of navigating your relationship together.

You're Not Alone

No family is "normal." What does "a normal family" even mean, anyway? Most adults are dealing with some family conflict or challenge in one form or another, and having a complicated relationship with your mother may just be one of yours.

That said, things don't have to remain the same. You don't have to stay stuck in the same old troubling patterns. My hope is that the tips in this book will help you make some changes in your life that move it in a positive direction. You can hopefully start by trying to understand the parts of your mother that are unique and wonderful that may have been harder to see before.

Prompts for Self-Reflection

- In what ways am I similar to or different from my siblings?
- What have I learned in this chapter that I could apply to any of my familial relationships?

Key Takeaways

- You likely hold a role in your immediate family that was influenced by your mother's autism. That role may or may not have evolved since childhood.
- Siblings sometimes share your experiences, which can be uplifting and helpful as you process your childhood. However, some relationships may not be as easy, as each person has different memories and experiences from childhood.
- If you picked up traits from your family members or situations that aren't serving you now, you have the power to change them.
- Your feelings around your childhood are valid, no matter what they are. Building capacity to make room for all your complex feelings about your childhood may also make more space for you to appreciate the expressions of love that you did experience.
- It may help to seek outside support through individual therapy and/or an experienced, neurodiversity-affirming family therapist, preferably one who specializes in working with adult families.

Moving Forward Together:

Strengthening Connection and Love with Your Mom

Learning more about autism in the framework of a mother-child relationship can be eye-opening and hugely beneficial. It can give context to key childhood memories, spark positive change, and remind you of the best parts of your relationship. It makes sense to think a lot about your childhood with this new lens, but it's also important to look ahead and know that improvements are possible. With a foundation of love and respect, you and your mother can strengthen your understanding of each other and find ways to forge meaningful connection.

Acknowledging Dual Truths

Working on your relationship with your mother can be both rewarding and stressful, inspiring and painful. Like so many things in adulthood, it's complicated. Multiple things can and will exist together at the same time. As we discussed in Chapter 2, Both/And Thinking can give you a framework for processing those moments. For example, you may have a new appreciation for how your mother's brain is wired and how she likely experiences the world . . . but you may also still have a lot of pain and confusion about how you experienced your childhood and now your adulthood with your mom. Both feelings are valid.

Accepting two opposing feelings simultaneously can help you make space in your mind and heart for some minor discomforts along the way. On one hand, you probably won't be able to reconcile every disparate preference or avoid every conflict—but on the other, you *will* be able to approach situations thoughtfully and give yourselves the best chance for success. Living in this duality can be tricky at first, but as you practice identifying the different factors at play, it will become more comfortable. Remember to also use the Double-Empathy Theory to reinforce that both parties should work together to build this connection.

Finding Compassion—for Both of You

Thinking about concepts like sensory processing, executive functioning, emotional expression, and energy levels within the framework of autism will help you better understand your mother's lived experience. For example, you may see your mom's adherence to routines and reduced flexibility as coping mechanisms, or strategies to support her functioning in the world rather than a form of rejection or rigidity. This mindset can naturally lead to greater compassion for both you and your mother.

Using this lens still may be hard work, and I'm not suggesting that you rewrite history and gloss over difficult parts of your life thus far. What is very helpful is finding a softer, kinder view of yourself and your mother, and maybe realizing that her choices and behaviors weren't done out of a lack of love. You might be able to find compassion, and try to be a person who supports your mom's differences, demonstrates flexibility and adaptability with her needs, and has a new respect for the complexity of being human. You might now also have the capacity and the language to have more thoughtful conversations with your mother. *All* relationships still require boundaries and clear discussion around each person's needs, so this is a useful skill in all areas of your life. You may now be able to structure your time together with your mom in different ways that feel good to you both too.

When Distance Is Best

Sometimes even after a lot of effort, it becomes clear that you are better off not having a close relationship with your mother. That's okay too, and many people choose that path. There is no easy or right answer. What's most important is that you feel safe and supported in your choice.

Relationships are complicated. The effort it takes to maintain healthy bonds isn't always easy, but it may be worth it if you are able to build a closer connection with your mom. Offer compassion for your younger self, your current self, and your future self as you continue to grow and evolve. If possible, share that compassion with your mother as well.

Look for Progress, Not Perfection

When reflecting on the progress you and your mom have made, try not to be frustrated if everything isn't perfect. Be proud of the progress you have made and celebrate wins along the way. Ask yourself:

- What things feel better than they used to?
- What did I learn that was most surprising?
- What changes have been easy to implement?
- What still feels painful?

Keep in mind that progress is often not linear. You may have days where things feel clearer and better understood, and days when everyone is getting on each other's nerves. Guess what? You and your mother are human. These are very normal human feelings and experiences.

Reading this book demonstrates your curiosity and commitment to understanding yourself and your relationship with your mother. Those ingredients can help you move forward with new awareness, new language, and a new perspective on your bond.

Additional Resources

Organizations

Association for Autism and Neurodiversity (AANE)

https://aane.org

AANE supports neurodivergent people and their families with education, support services, and community building.

Autistic Self Advocacy Network

https://autisticadvocacy.org

A group run by and for Autistic people that promotes rights of people with disabilities and provides resources.

Boston University's ASD Women's Group

www.instagram.com/bu.asdwomensgroup/

This account shares resources and tools for women.

RaisedByAutistics Reddit Community

www.reddit.com/r/raisedbyautistics/

A space for those who have been (or suspect they have been) raised by Autistic parents to share personal experiences and emotional support.

Journal Articles

"Invisible Girls: Is Autism Being Overlooked in Girls Because the Signs Are Much Clearer in Boys? A Growing Body of Research Says Yes" by Nancy Volkers, *The ASHA Leader*, Volume 23, Number 4, 48–55 (2018).
https://leader.pubs.asha.org/doi/10.1044/leader.FTR1.23042018.48

A brief description of why girls are often overlooked.

"The Female Autism Phenotype and Camouflaging: A Narrative Review" by Laura Hull, K.V. Petrides, and William Mandy, *Review Journal of Autism and Developmental Disorders*, Volume 7, 306–317 (2020).
https://link.springer.com/article/10.1007/s40489-020-00197-9

A scientific look at what Autistic females can present, with a description of "masking."

Videos

"What Women with Autism Want You to Know" by Iris (2018).
https://youtu.be/NwEH9Ui4HV8?si=r_JlUECOdAOXYDmC

Various Autistic women talk about their experiences and debunk public misconceptions.

"Why Everything You Know about Autism Is Wrong" by Jac den Houting at TEDxMacquarieUniversity (2019).
https://youtu.be/A1AUdaH-EPM?si=GwI31gbDJkd3p14m

An Autistic researcher shares her experience and how she is trying to improve Autistic research and convey why what you think about Autism isn't necessarily accurate.

TV Shows/Films

These are various media options that share authentic depictions of autism.

Mildly Different

Atypical

Temple Grandin

Love on the Spectrum

As We See It

Books

***Autistic Burnout Workbook: Your Guide to Your Personal Recovery Plan* by Dr. Megan Anna Neff**

A book that was created by a neurodivergent (Autistic-ADHD) clinician, parent, and advocate to provide support around understanding and combating Autistic burnout.

***Sensory: Life on the Spectrum* by Bex Ollerton**

A collection of comics by autistic creators exploring diverse experiences with autism, from diagnosis to daily life, sensory overload, and finding community.

***Thinking in Pictures: My Life with Autism* by Temple Grandin**

Written by an Autistic woman, this book describes her life experience.

***Unmasking Autism* and *Unmasking for Life* by Dr. Devon Price**

Thoughtful guides to unmasking, advocating for yourself, and embracing your identity.

Finding Neurodivergent Therapists

Neurodivergent Insights
https://neurodivergentinsights.com

A community that creates "research-informed AuDHD, autism, and ADHD resources, grounded in clinical insight and lived experience."

Neurodivergent Therapists
https://ndtherapists.com

Search to find neurodivergent-affirming care.

The Neurodiversity Collective
www.theneurodiversitycollective.com

Website created by an Autistic speech-language pathologist for supports around neurodiversity-affirming care.

Index